Start Your Own

CONSULTING BUSINESS

Additional titles in *Entrepreneur's* **Startup Series**

Start Your Own

Entrepreneur
MAGAZINE'S

*start*up

3RD EDITION

Start Your Own

CONSULTING BUSINESS

*Your Step-by-Step
Guide to Success*

Entrepreneur Press

EP
Entrepreneur.
Press

Publisher: Jere L. Calmes
Cover Design: Beth Hansen-Winter
Production and Composition: CWL Publishing Enterprises, Inc., Madison, WI,
www.cwlpub.com

This publication is designed to provide accurate and authoritative information in regard
to the subject matter covered. It is sold with the understanding that the publisher is not
engaged in rendering legal, accounting or other professional services. If legal advice or
other expert assistance is required, the services of a competent professional person
should be sought.

ISBN 13: 978-1-59918-373-2
       10: 159918-373-0

Library of Congress Cataloging-in-Publication available

Printed in Canada
14 13   10 9 8 7 6 5 4 3

Contents

▲

Preface

If you've been dreaming of leaving your current job to become the chief executive officer of your own small business, you're retired and want to put your knowledge and talents to work in a new business, or you just want to earn some extra money on the side, then you've come to the right place. The book you're holding is your personal roadmap to becoming a self-employed entrepreneur in your own consulting business. It touches on all the groundwork you'll need to do to set up that business, from selecting a business name to obtaining business licenses, drumming up work, wrangling financing, and more—tasks that are just as necessary for success as your talents and skills will be when you finally hang out your shingle on that first day on the job.

And that day could be pretty scary. After all, you won't be getting a paycheck on the following Friday. You won't have co-workers to commiserate with, or a support staff to cater to your every whim. In fact, possibly for the first time you'll be handling tasks you've never done before, like one consultant we know, who said, "I ran a corporate business, but a lot of things were done automatically for me. I truly didn't understand [things like] profit and loss statements vs. cash flow statements because I had financial people who worried about those things for me."

We can help. This book contains information on all the major tasks you'll encounter on the road to successful self-employment, including the 411 you need on:

- Assessing your skills and defining your market
- Selecting a legal form of operation and naming your business
- Finding business professionals to help run the show
- Setting up your home office
- Managing daily administrative tasks
- Hiring personnel (something that could happen sooner than you think)
- Locating professional development resources
- Prospecting for clients and promoting your business
- Establishing an internet presence
- Financing the business and staying in the black
- And much more

So no matter whether your consulting business will focus on human resources placement, computer troubleshooting, public relations, meeting planning, or anything else you can dream up, you're about to join the other 10.4 million people in the United States who have decided to seek their fame and fortune armed only with their own talents, capabilities, ambition, and determination.

Enjoy the ride.

Start Your Own

CONSULTING BUSINESS

1

The Right
Stuff

What exactly is a consultant? The word comes from the Latin word for "to discuss," while the dictionary defines *consultant* as "an expert in a particular field who works as an advisor either to a company or to another individual." Sounds pretty vague, doesn't it? But interestingly it's that very vagueness that gives you the leeway to create a consulting business that's exactly what you want it to be and allows you to do precisely what you want to do.

Businesses certainly understand the value of consultants. According to estimates by Plunkett Research, a provider of industry sector analysis and research, management, scientific, and technical consulting services generated more than $160 billion in revenues in the United States during 2007, while Kennedy Information, a leading source of research for professionals in the management, IT consulting, executive recruiting, and investor relations professions, reports that worldwide consulting revenues were $310 billion.

That's a pretty good indication that the market is wide open for new consultants in virtually every industry.

And there's more good news. The Bureau of Labor Statistics (BLS), U.S. Department of Labor, Career Guide to Industries, reports:

- The management, scientific, and technical consulting industry will rank among the fastest-growing over the next decade.
- Consulting is one of the highest-paying industries around.
- Consultants are highly educated (74 percent have a bachelor's degree or higher).

But why exactly are consultants in such high demand? First, companies understand the value consultants bring to their organizations by virtue of their experience, expertise, and knowledge. Second, consultants bring fresh ideas and a fresh perspective to projects. And third, companies that have to lay off workers for economic reasons still need to get the work done despite their reduced labor pool.

Taking the Plunge

For their part, independent consultants have different motivations for taking the plunge into self-employment. Some of them are baby boomers who may have worked for years—or decades—for one or more companies, and simply are ready for a career that will allow them to call the shots for a change. Others, like Bill Metten, a consultant in Hockessin, Delaware, have been laid off or downsized out of a job and decided to seek a new opportunity that will allow them to use the knowledge they've acquired on the job.

"I was a senior executive for a chemical company when the industry went to pot in the early 1990s," says Metten, who founded his public relations/customer service consulting business in 1991. "The company made me an offer I couldn't refuse, and since I had long harbored the desire to have just a few clients and spoil the dickens out of them, I decided to take the plunge."

And still others, like Melinda Patrician, a public relations consultant in Arlington, Virginia, discovered that technology made it easier to work as a consultant from home.

"The same technology that has helped me to be successful as a consultant has made it easier for others to do the same," Patrician says.

Simply put, a consultant's job is to consult. It really is that simple. But what separates a good consultant from a bad consultant is a passion and drive for excellence. And of course, good consultants should be knowledgeable about the subjects they're consulting in. You see, in this day and age, anyone can be a consultant in pretty much any field or discipline, from management to wedding coordination, academic course design, professional image, interior design, and much more. All you need to discover is what your particular gift is. For example, are you proficient with computers, by virtue of your job history or personal interests? Do you keep up with the latest in software and hardware, and have the latest and greatest equipment on your own desktop? Are you well versed in web design, blogging, and social networking? And are you able to take the knowledge you've gained and turn it into a resource that someone would be willing to pay money for? Then you could be an awesome computer consultant.

Or maybe you're an expert in the fundraising field. Maybe you've worked for nonprofit agencies in marketing, public relations, or sales, and over the years you've discovered the secret of raising vats of money. It's possible to turn that kind of fundraising success into a lucrative consulting business, according to John Riddle, a fundraising consultant in Bear, Delaware, who has done just that. Fundraising is growing in small social services agencies, such as soup kitchens and homeless shelters, and in large universities, colleges, and nonprofit hospitals. So once you've successfully learned how to write grant proposals to foundations and corporations and gotten a few years of experience under your belt, you could join the ranks of fundraising consultants who are earning six-figure salaries—or even more.

> **Tip...**
>
> **Smart Tip**
> Before you decide on a consulting specialty, make sure you have a passion for that field. If you can imagine talking with someone for hours at a time about your specialty without referring to notes or books, then you clearly have selected the right field in which to work as a consultant.

And in case you're wondering, yes, it is possible to be a consultant in more than one field at the same time. Riddle did this, when he simultaneously built a successful fundraising consulting business while using his writing skills to develop an editorial consulting business. But while this sounds like a great way to earn income fast, it did have its pitfalls. It wasn't unusual for Riddle to find himself meeting with the board of directors of a nonprofit agency concerning fundraising strategies one day, and the next day show-

> **⚠ Beware!**
> If you decide to consult in more than one field, be certain that you can devote enough time and energy to both; otherwise, you run the risk of having both of your consulting specialties fail.

'Tis the Reason

Although money often is a key factor when someone decides to become a consultant, there are a few other reasons why people choose this profession:

- *You're not living your dream.* Maybe your dream has been to work on your own and to be your own boss. As a consultant, you're responsible for your career, not someone else's.
- *You're about to lose your job (or have already).* Job security is almost a thing of the past, as everyone knows. Gone are the days when you work for the same company for 20 or 30 years, receive your gold watch, and spend your retirement fishing. As a consultant, you have the power to control your economic future—and ultimate happiness.
- *You have a talent people will pay money for.* Suppose you worked for 20 years in a particular profession—say, fundraising or financial management or event planning—and built a reputation for yourself. Odds are, people will pay you for that knowledge and skill.
- *You want an additional source of income.* Maybe your goal or desire is to work only part-time as a consultant. Many consultants in this country are successfully supplementing their incomes by practicing on the side. Be advised, however, if your consulting business begins to interfere with your main job, you may have to choose between the two.
- *You believe you can make a difference.* Many people become consultants because they know they can do a particular job better than someone else. If you believe in something, nothing should stand in your way!

ing a client how to break into the publishing world by writing book reviews for a local newspaper. But the truth is, taking on so much when you first launch a business can be exhausting, and Riddle himself confesses that at times he wished he had concentrated on one or the other field and not felt so compelled to work in different areas. Keep that in mind if you find yourself being pulled in too many directions when you start your own consulting business.

Smart Tip

Tip...

Come up with a list of your own short- and long-term goals, and write them down on paper. Review them, and revise them regularly. By having your goals written down, you'll be more likely to meet them.

Things to Consider

When it comes right down to it, working as a consultant can be exciting and lucrative. Where else can you work as a self-employed independent operator, set your own hours, and even set your own fees? Of course, you must be willing to devote the time and effort it takes to make a living as a consultant; otherwise, your consulting business will face significant challenges that could sink it even before it gets off the ground.

Consulting is not for the faint of heart, says Huntington Beach, California, human resources consultant Susan Bock, and a past president of the Association of Professional Consultants. "This is not the business arena for someone who enjoys predictability," she says. "There are no two days or months that are exactly the same, which can be intimidating for some people. But for someone who loves the freedom of working with his or her own clients, it's a wonderful life, and one that allows for exponential personal and professional growth."

When considering starting a consulting business, first ask yourself:

- *What certifications and special licensing will I need?* Depending on your profession, you may need special certification or a license before you can begin operating as a consultant. For example, fundraising consultants don't need special certification, although you can become certified through the Association of Fund Raising Professionals. And in some states, you may need to register as a professional fundraising consultant before starting your business.

- *Am I qualified to become a consultant?* Before you hang out your shingle and hope that clients will begin beating down your door to hire you, make sure you have the qualifications necessary to get the job done. If you want to be a computer consultant, for example, make sure you are up to date in the knowledge department with all the trends and changes in the computer industry.

- *Am I organized enough to become a consultant?* Do I like to plan my day? Am I an expert when it comes to time management? You should have answered yes to both of those questions!

- *Do I like to network?* Networking is critical to the success of any type of consultant today. Begin building your network of contacts immediately.

- *Have I set long- and short-term goals? How do they help me become a consultant?* If your goals don't match up with the time and energy it takes to open and successfully build a consulting business, then reconsider before moving in this direction.

Do You Have What It Takes?

While just about anybody can be a consultant, the best ones possess some important skills, including:

- *Listening skills:* When people talk, do you listen? This may sound like an easy

Things to Consider

When it comes right down to it, working as a consultant can be exciting and lucrative. Where else can you work as a self-employed independent operator, set your own hours, and even set your own fees? Of course, you must be willing to devote the time and effort it takes to make a living as a consultant; otherwise, your consulting business will face significant challenges that could sink it even before it gets off the ground.

Consulting is not for the faint of heart, says Huntington Beach, California, human resources consultant Susan Bock, and a past president of the Association of Professional Consultants. "This is not the business arena for someone who enjoys predictability," she says. "There are no two days or months that are exactly the same, which can be intimidating for some people. But for someone who loves the freedom of working with his or her own clients, it's a wonderful life, and one that allows for exponential personal and professional growth."

When considering starting a consulting business, first ask yourself:

- *What certifications and special licensing will I need?* Depending on your profession, you may need special certification or a license before you can begin operating as a consultant. For example, fundraising consultants don't need special certification, although you can become certified through the Association of Fund Raising Professionals. And in some states, you may need to register as a professional fundraising consultant before starting your business.

- *Am I qualified to become a consultant?* Before you hang out your shingle and hope that clients will begin beating down your door to hire you, make sure you have the qualifications necessary to get the job done. If you want to be a computer consultant, for example, make sure you are up to date in the knowledge department with all the trends and changes in the computer industry.

- *Am I organized enough to become a consultant?* Do I like to plan my day? Am I an expert when it comes to time management? You should have answered yes to both of those questions!

- *Do I like to network?* Networking is critical to the success of any type of consultant today. Begin building your network of contacts immediately.

- *Have I set long- and short-term goals? How do they help me become a consultant?* If your goals don't match up with the time and energy it takes to open and successfully build a consulting business, then reconsider before moving in this direction.

Do You Have What It Takes?

While just about anybody can be a consultant, the best ones possess some important skills, including:

- *Listening skills:* When people talk, do you listen? This may sound like an easy

▲

question, but listening is an acquired skill. By carefully listening to your clients' needs, you'll be able to better solve their problems.

- *Investigative skills:* You need to have the ability to investigate and uncover the data necessary to complete your consulting assignment. And it takes more than just good Googling skills—you also need an analytical mind, creativity, patience, and perseverance.

- *Analytical skills:* When you investigate and uncover data, you had better know what it means! Your ability to understand and analyze complex information relative to your consulting field is paramount to success.

- *Change skills:* You must be a person who embraces change and who can persuade your clients to make the changes necessary to solve their problems.

- *Action skills:* A good consultant must be ready to do whatever it takes to get the job done, when it needs to be done, including the weekends, holidays, or when you'd rather be in Maui combing the beach for seashells.

> **Bright Idea**
> Make a list of the top 10 reasons why a business should hire you as a consultant. This will help you when you prepare your marketing strategy and pitch your services to clients.

You'll learn more about the day-to-day responsibilities of running a consulting business in Chapter 2.

A Brief History of Consulting

It wasn't until the 1950s that consultants began to emerge in the business world. Until then, consultants could be found in the legal, finance, and employment fields. Then in the early 1960s, the U.S. economy changed from production- to service-oriented, which proved to be the perfect incubator for a new comprehensive consulting industry. Happily, by positioning themselves as experts in their particular fields, consultants found themselves in great demand by companies that needed help but couldn't justify increasing their payroll to get it.

Then during the economic recession of the late 1970s and early 1980s, corporate America suddenly found it difficult to turn a profit. There seemed to be no other way to boost the bottom line other than by reducing staff. So little by little, businesses began to cut back on operating costs by offering early retirement packages to long-term employees and laying off anyone they felt was expendable.

From a corporate point of view, the thinking was simply "It makes sense to hire a consultant," since paying a consultant seemed like a cost-effective means of doing business. So not only was there a boost in the demand for consultants, but also many people who had accepted early retirement packages were now setting up shop as consultants, often working for the very businesses that had let them go. At the same time, many consultants were faced with a dilemma most people never have to face: too much business! So rather than turn away a client, independent consultants joined with other consultants in their field, and thus the consulting industry was born.

According to industry experts, here are the top 10 reasons organizations hire consultants:

1. *A consultant has the right expertise.* This is where it pays not only to be really good in your chosen field, but also to have a track record that speaks for itself. For example, Riddle says he knows that every client who hired him did so partly on the basis of his track record. After all, if your nonprofit organization needs to raise $1 million, it makes sense to hire someone who has already raised millions for other organizations.

2. *A consultant may be hired to identify problems.* Sometimes employees are too close to a problem inside an organization to identify it. That's when a consultant rides in on his or her white horse to save the day.

3. *A consultant can supplement the staff.* Sometimes a business discovers it can save thousands of dollars a week by hiring consultants when they are needed rather than hiring full-time employees. They also can save additional money because they don't have to pay benefits to the consultants they hire. Even though a consultant's fees are generally higher than an employee's salary, over the long haul it makes good economic sense to hire a consultant.

4. *A consultant can act as a catalyst for change.* No one likes change, especially corporate America. But sometimes change is needed, and a consultant may be brought in to implement the changes. A benefit to the company is that the consultant can do things without worrying about the corporate culture, employee morale, or other issues that get in the way when an organization is trying to institute change.

5. *A consultant provides much-needed objectivity.* Who else is more qualified to identify a problem than a consultant? A good consultant provides an objective, fresh viewpoint without worrying about what people in the organization might think about the results and how they were achieved.

6. *A consultant may be hired to teach.* Consultants are called on to teach many skills. Of course, it's the consultant's task to keep up with developments in their field of expertise so they're always ready to teach new clients what they need to stay competitive.

7. *A consultant may be hired to do the "dirty work."* Let's face it: No one wants to be the person who has to make cuts in the staff or to eliminate an entire division. An impartial outside consultant is the perfect person to handle such unpleasant tasks.

▲

8. *A consultant can bring new life to an organization.* If you're good at coming up with ideas that work, then you won't have any trouble finding clients. At one time or another, most businesses need someone to administer "first aid" to get things rolling again.

9. *A consultant may be hired to create a new business.* There are consultants who are experts in this discipline. But it does require special skill, so make sure you have it before you market yourself as a business development consultant.

10. *A consultant may be hired to influence other people.* Do you like to hang out with the rich and famous in your town? If so, you may be hired to do a consulting job based on whom you know.

Tip...

Smart Tip
A consultant needs to be a good listener. So the next time you're in a conversation, resist the urge to interrupt with questions or your own comments until the other person has completely finished talking.

! Beware!
Before accepting any consulting assignment, be certain that the potential client isn't involved in any litigation concerning employment discrimination practices.

The Top Consulting Businesses

Although you can consult in just about any field these days, Attard Communications, a small, homebased business consulting firm, says that the types of consulting businesses that are thriving today include:

- *Accounting:* Businesses of all sizes—and especially small businesses—need everything from bookkeeping to tax preparation, making this a solid career choice for a new consultant.

- *Advertising:* An advertising consultant may be needed to develop strategic ad campaigns, write copy, and make ad buys, in some cases.

- *Career:* Widespread corporate downsizing has created a need for consultants who can help jobseekers reinvent themselves, polish their resumes, and otherwise make themselves irresistible to employers.

- *Computer consulting:* Consultants who are well versed in web page and blog development, software and hardware installation and troubleshooting, internet marketing, and other things cyber-based can build a viable business.

- *Education:* From finding scholarship money and advising kids who are writing their college applications, to assisting school districts with budgetary issues and other matters, an education consultant may find her- or himself in great demand these days.

- *Executive search:* No matter whether the economy is in recession or booming, headhunters (aka executive search consultants) are always in demand.

- *Human resources:* Corporations often need help with personnel issues like conflict resolution, violence in the workplace, sexual harassment awareness, and other people matters—not to mention those downsizing issues mentioned earlier.

- *Insurance:* Advising people about their insurance needs and finding the best policies at the best price remains a field with strong opportunities for new consultants.

- *Management:* Fresh ideas on how to manage a business better are always in demand, especially when a company is facing challenging economic times.

- *Public relations:* Companies thrive on press coverage that puts them in the best possible light, and the consultant who has the tools and contacts to get such coverage can be invaluable.

Other fields with strong possibilities for fledgling consultants include corporate communications, graphic design, editorial writing, marketing, motivational speaking, payroll management, strategic planning, and tax advising.

More Keys to Success

Finally, to be a successful consultant, you must be a successful entrepreneur—someone who's creative, freethinking, independent, and brave enough to take calculated risks. Erin Blaskie, an author, motivational speaker, and internet marketing specialist at BSETC (bsetc.ca), offers these guidelines for becoming a successful entrepreneur:

- *Implement ideas fast.* "Don't hold back and don't dilly-dally with details and with trying to be perfect," she says. "Get your ideas out there and tweak as you go."

- *Use your strengths, and delegate the rest:* Don't try to do everything yourself. Let's face it—to be successful, you need to learn that you aren't the best person to do everything in your business. Read *The E-Myth Revisited* by Michael Gerber for a great take on what it means to wear many hats as an entrepreneur. It'll make you realize that you should focus on what you're good at and then delegate the rest. Find the right people, and they'll pay for themselves.

- *Surround yourself with a good support system.* Learn to surround yourself with positive people, and rid yourself of toxic people.

▲

- *Do only what you love.* Never do anything you don't love to do. Why not? You run the risk of doing a poor job at it or taking light years to turn things around. Humans aren't meant to do everything; we're meant to do the work where our passion lies and where our heart is, because *that's* what makes us successful.

- *Work only with people who energize you.* Find clients who inspire and energize you, who embrace your talents, and who understand the way you work.

- *Limit your overhead.* Stay in the green, and you'll become more successful. Think of how much less stress you'll have when money isn't an issue!

- *Be generous.* Don't be afraid to give away information or help out fellow business-people for nothing in return. It feels great, and people will remember you. Dr. Linda Henman, a strategy coach in St. Louis and author of The Magnetic Boss, offers one more crucial piece of advice: "In general, you should have three years of living expenses in savings because a great load of money goes out the door during the three to five years it will take you to launch, and not much comes in," she says. "If you don't have a cushion, you'll be tempted to set your fees too low, which is the #1 mistake consultants make and often the kiss of death."

Earnings Potential

By now, you must be wondering just how much money you can earn in your new consulting career. The answer is: There's no way of knowing until you start earning it. The income depends on the type of industry you're serving (for example, aerospace engineering pays more than education consulting), your location (major metropolitan areas have higher pay scales), and your experience in your field (people pay for know-how).

But you don't have to take it on faith that it's possible to earn a good living as a consultant. The BLS says there were nearly 536,000 consultants in 2008 who had a mean annual wage of $82,980. By comparison, the mean annual wage for management, scientific, and technical consultants was $96,420, while the mean annual wage for computer systems design and related consultants was $88,030. And those figures represent people who were employees of firms, not self-employed consultants as you aspire to be. The BLS says the earnings of independent consultants have the potential to be even higher.

> **Fun Fact**
> The word *entrepreneur* comes from two French words: *entre,* meaning "between," and *prendre,* meaning "to take." As a consultant, you'll be entering into new ventures and taking new risks—and *voilà!* That makes you an entrepreneur in the truest sense of the word.

Quittin' Time

Before you decide to open up shop, think carefully about why you want to become a consultant. It's important that you don't become a consultant for the wrong reasons. For example, if you and your boss aren't getting along, but you've had differences with him or her in the past and have always reached an understanding, then you probably don't want to leave your job and become a consultant. However, if you're really dissatisfied with your boss and your company and can envision doing the work more efficiently on your own, then you're probably a good candidate for starting your own business.

Carol Monaco, a Brighton, Colorado, market research consultant, concurs. "I know consultants who earn $400,000—and others who earn $20,000," Monaco says. "It all depends on how much effort you put into it."

Bringing Your
Specialty to Market

Ask any consultant—or the successful one, anyway—why he or she decided to start a consulting practice, and you're likely to hear that it was because that person had a particular skill or knowledge that others would find useful. That knowledge might be about anything from health-care marketing to trade show management; jewelry manufacturing to process development—not to mention whatever skill

▲

or knowledge you personally have. The fact is, any professional knowledge you've acquired in life—whether in traditional job settings or through educational pursuits—potentially can be turned into a value-added service for a client. The trick is to play up that knowledge to its best advantage. This chapter helps you specialize for success. We examine ways to determine how to analyze your own skills as a way to turn your specialty into a career, as well as how to identify the right market for your services that will help you specialize for success.

What's Your Specialty?

It's important to give this a lot of thought before you plunge into a consulting career. One reason why consultants are respected and sought after is because they are perceived as experts in their fields. It's also the reason why companies will pay the big bucks for their insights and experience. Your mission must be to position yourself as that expert—and to start that process, you need to identify, in an honest and unbiased fashion, the specialized skills you have.

One way to do this is to make up a personal skills inventory. In doing so, consider what you like and don't like to do, both personally and professionally, since all insights are valuable in determining your career path.

Here's what the inventory for a fictitious special event planner might look like:

- *Things I excel at:* Special event and space planning, process engineering, researching, writing, sales, public relations, promotion
- *Useful skills I possess:* Knack for customer service, typing, photography, space planning, ability to describe complex processes in plain English, interior design
- *Concepts/processes/procedures I have in-depth knowledge about:* Contract negotiation, space planning, personnel management, motivation
- *Things I'd rather be doing:* Planning destination weddings, writing, teaching workshops, dancing with the stars, sitting on a beach in Maui, volcano watching
- *Things wild horses couldn't make me do:* Computer troubleshooting, writing poetry, planning and organizing conventions

You'll notice that some items appear more than once in the inventory in one form or another. If that happens when you make your own list, consider that an insight into where you should start when you explore your options for creating a profession you will love. If there isn't any overlap, you may need to take some classes or get some experience in your chosen activity before you make the leap into employment.

In the meantime, try your hand at creating your own skills inventory by using the worksheet you'll find on page 22.

Now that you've noted your skills, make a list of every one you have that might be useful to a generic consulting client. (Don't worry about targeting your list just yet.)

Some may include:

- Advising people
- Analyzing financial information
- Brainstorming
- Chunking information
- Coordinating details
- Finding solutions
- Interpreting statistics
- Making oral presentations
- Managing people
- Motivating/coaching individuals and teams
- Raising funds
- Researching information
- Selling products or ideas
- Teaching
- Writing reports

You probably have far more skills than just these. For more ideas, Google "skills assessment" or "skills inventory" to find lists you can use as idea-starters.

Now in a perfect world, you would take all these skills, scramble them up, and reassemble them like a jigsaw puzzle to create a perfect match with a client company. But that's not your goal here. Rather, you want to identify exactly what it is that you do well so you don't take on jobs at which you can't excel. And you'll be tempted to do that, especially when you're starting your business and revenues are low. But be forewarned—if you accept work from a client and don't perform to expectation, the word will get around and your consulting career could sink faster than you can say, "Man overboard."

Once you've compiled your skills inventory, consider the industries that would benefit most from your skills and abilities. Naturally, you'll want to start with the industries in which you have experience. For example, if you've been employed as a computer consultant in the insurance industry, you'll definitely want to pitch your computer services to that industry. From there, consider related industries that might have possibilities. That computer consultant, for instance, definitely should consider approaching companies that process insurance claim forms, as well as financial institutions, since they often offer insurance products to their customers as part of their services. Now, does it matter that the computer consultant knows little or nothing about insurance psychobabble, like acceleration clauses and reinsurance? Nope—because the service he will be selling revolves around programming computers, creating websites, and performing routine maintenance tasks, not selling insurance or interpreting the psychobabble. The point is, use your previous experience in the field as a foot in the door of related industries.

Of course, this doesn't mean that you shouldn't pursue jobs in other industries, too. It's just a good idea to start with a narrow, targeted swath of the business universe rather than using a scattershot approach to landing clients.

Newark, Delaware consultant Merrily Schiavone adroitly used this narrow, targeted marketing approach to drum up business when she parlayed her expertise as a newspaper advertising salesperson into a new career as a consultant. It

Smart Tip

> Tip...

You'll be more successful if you focus on serving a single industry when you launch your business, according to Boulder, Colorado, market research consultant Carol Monaco (marketwise insights.com). "The advantage of targeting rather than being a generalist is that you'll find it easier to explain what you do, and your business will get started faster as a result," she says.

all started when she found herself giving advice to her newspaper clients on how to market their business better.

"I actually started getting clients while I was selling newspaper ad space, and I quickly realized that was a conflict of interest," Schiavone explains. "So I started a one-person advertising agency."

Beware!

Don't confuse something you like to do in your spare time with a field of expertise. Hobbies rarely translate into viable consulting businesses. Likewise, don't choose such an obscure specialty that you'll find it difficult to find clients. Be sure to do some research and make sure there's a market for your chosen consulting field.

Sometimes, just thinking outside the box can help you land in a great new profession, as John Riddle, the fundraising consultant in Bear, Delaware, did. He was working in a payroll department when he discovered that one of his true passions was writing. So after seven years in a job he hated, he went to work for a small public relations firm where he did some promotional writing and event planning. Eventually he started teaching workshops and published newsletters to show people how to break into the world of freelance writing. He has continued to use that communications and public relations experience in his career as a fundraising consultant.

However, one thing you shouldn't do is to attempt to be all things to all people. And as mentioned earlier, you'll be tempted, especially in the early days of your new career.

"This is a struggle every emerging consultant faces," says Huntington Beach, California human resources consultant Susan Bock. "Being desperate for success, new

Bright Idea

While not every hobby can be turned into a successful consulting business, some actually can make the cut. For example, if you collect antiques, you could use your knowledge of the antiques industry to provide appraisal services.

consultants tend to say yes to everything. But this is the biggest disservice you can do to yourself. Always be very clear about what you can and want to do, and the business will come."

Defining Your Market

You've determined that you have the right experience and you've got something to offer. Here's the next important thing to consider: Your idea may be the best one you've ever thought of, but there needs to be a market for your ideas. In other words, someone must be willing and able to pay you for your expert advice.

So here are some thoughts to ponder: Who is your target audience and who are your potential clients? Will you be marketing your consulting services to large corporations? Will your specialty interest only smaller businesses? Or would you like to focus only on nonprofit organizations? You need to consider these questions before you start consulting so you get your business off on the right foot (i.e., the one that moves it forward successfully).

Smart Tip

Since the consulting business is all about people, use every opportunity available to develop a relationship with the people you're working for. Be someone they will come to depend on now and in the future.

Case in point: Bock realized early on that she preferred working with smaller companies, which prompted her to target her efforts toward only that size of business. "Working with larger organizations is like trying to turn the Titanic," she says. "Smaller companies—and especially women-owned companies—appealed to me because I can understand and appreciate the issues of both small businesses and women. I also like immediate gratification, which you can't get working with a big company."

"I'm a strong believer in identifying a target market," adds Carol Monaco, a Boulder, Colorado market research consultant. "The better you target, the better you'll be able to sell your services. In fact, when clients come to me for help because they're struggling, I always ask who their target market is. If they say, 'Everyone,' I know right away where the problem is."

Writing a Marketing Plan

You can head off such problems by viewing your market realistically, then targeting your services to the right people. One methodical and sensible way to go about doing that is to prepare a marketing plan, which will become part of your overall business plan (something we'll get to in Chapter 4). The goal of a marketing plan is to discuss in detail the steps you'll take to bring a product—or in your case, a service—to the market. There's a simple reason for spending time writing such a plan.

"You need a roadmap showing where you're going," Monaco says emphatically. "A marketing plan will help you determine how you want to grow your business and where the business is headed, which is important because you can't just put out your shingle and hope people will flock to you. It just doesn't happen that way."

According to the SBA, a marketing plan should include:

- *A description of your business:* Define what you plan to do, where you'll do it (in a geographical location, in cyberspace, etc.), and who is your competition.

- *Current information about the marketplace:* You need to know who's currently buying your services, how much in demand they are, and what the prospects are for future sales. At this point, it's enough to talk in generalities—when you write your business plan, you can be more specific.

- *A description of your customers:* Consider everyone from the CEOs at Fortune 500 companies to small-business owners. Also give some thought to your customer pool's demographics, which are the various characteristics that define the group. Demographics you'll want to consider include age, income, occupation, gender, and marital status. To understand why this is important, imagine that you plan to offer consulting services for a simple task like helping people to download tunes to their iPods. To make this business a success, you'd have to target your marketing efforts to people over the age of about 50, since younger folks generally are tech-savvy and unlikely to need this service. (In fact, they could be your competition!)

> **Bright Idea**
> Need more information and guidance on writing that all-important marketing plan? Visit the SBA at sba.gov, or go to our favorite website (entrepreneur.com) and search for "marketing plan." You can also find plenty of free marketing plan templates on the internet.

- *Specific strategies for business development and growth:* Here's where you'll note your plans for launching and growing your business, as well as the specific steps you'll take to make that happen.

- *Details about your budget:* Even if your budget is minuscule, you need to note exactly how you'll pay for this new venture and what you'll spend the money on.
- *Promotional strategies:* Be sure to discuss exactly how you'll promote your services to your target market. It's also helpful to create a timetable for implementation.
- *Business objectives:* This is an easy one—just make a list of exactly what you want to accomplish with this new venture. This can include anything from "landing five clients on retainer the first year," to "making a six-figure income in three years," to "landing a segment on Oprah and becoming the next Dr. Phil." OK, that last one probably isn't likely to happen, but you never know. It's important to have dreams, so write it down anyway.

When your marketing plan is polished and proofed, don't just stick it in a drawer—keep it handy and refer to it frequently. As time goes by, you'll want to update it to reflect your successes and outline your future plans.

Finding Prospects

Once you have all that background information in hand, you can begin the process of identifying specific people or groups of people who might need your services. The best place to start is in your field of expertise. For example, if you, like Riddle, decide to become a fundraising consultant, you could check to see which nonprofit organizations in your town hold fundraisers. They might need help making their fundraisers

Quality Check

Do you have what it takes to succeed as a consultant? Check out the top 10 qualities every good consultant possesses:

1. Intelligence
2. Flexibility
3. Critical thinking skills
4. Reliability
5. Resourcefulness
6. Excellent communication skills
7. Integrity
8. Perseverance
9. Sense of humor
10. Dedication

Be Outstanding in Your Field

If you want to score six-figure earnings, you need to become an outstanding consultant. But what makes a consultant outstanding? The best consultants strive to:

- *Eat, drink, and breathe customer service.* It may sound like a cliché, but outstanding consultants go the extra mile for their customers. That makes them memorable—and sought after.
- *Keep up with the latest changes in your field of expertise.* Read professional journals, attend workshops, and network with other people in your field.
- *Develop the ability to identify problems quickly.* Know what you're talking about. Clients hire you because of your expertise; don't disappoint them.
- *Look for creative ways to solve problems.* "Outside the box" thinking often reaps great rewards—and makes you look like a superstar!
- *Develop excellent communication skills.* Read, attend workshops, practice writing reports—whatever it takes to enhance your ability to communicate.
- *Be 100 percent confident that they'll succeed.* There's no room for uncertainty when you're doling out advice as a consultant. Be confident and positive, and you'll be in demand.
- *Be professional in everything they do.* Always look and sound like a polished professional, and you'll gain respect from your clients and peers.
- *Be a people person.* "I've learned that you need to get to know people personally and develop relationships to be a successful consultant," says Monaco. "People buy from people they like—and such relationships also make my life more interesting!"
- *Practice good management skills.* Good managers are experts at time management and do whatever it takes to get the job done.
- *Give clients more than they expect.* You'll be surprised at their response!

more successful. Or maybe they *don't* hold fundraisers because they don't know how to do it, or they're too understaffed to handle all the work involved. Both situations may be viewed as prime opportunities for a fundraising consultant. For more information on market research, check out the "If You Build It, Will They Come" chapter in *Startup Basics.*

Doing some simple market research is another good way to identify prospects, and you can do it at little or no cost. Monaco recommends surveying the journals in the field you're interested in to see who's advertising and what those companies are doing. You may find your capabilities are a good match with what they do, and you can then pitch

Bright Idea

Consider sending a survey to a variety of organizations you would like to have as clients. In your survey, ask if they have ever worked with a consultant in the past, and ask them to share as much fee information as possible. And don't forget to ask them if they were pleased with the consultant's performance and if they felt they received their money's worth.

your services to them. Other strategies for scoring free information include contacting industry experts; calling industry associations, which sometimes are willing to share the data they compile; contacting the local chamber of commerce; networking at business functions; and visiting U.S. government sites, like Census.gov and the Bureau of Labor Statistics. The latter offers useful demographic information at bls.gov/bls/demographics.htm.

Once you exhaust the free resources, don't hesitate to spend a few bucks for the information you still need. "Some information is just worth paying for, especially if you're planning to seek funding for your business," Monaco says. "Spending a little money on the right research will help you go down the right path, which is important because time is money."

⚠ Beware!

While the government has plenty of factoids and info tidbits at its disposal, the wheels of government turn slowly, so the information tends to be a few years old. But the data still can be useful for your preliminary market research efforts.

Skills Inventory Worksheet

1. Things I excel at:

   _____

   _____

   _____

2. Useful skills I possess:

   _____

   _____

   _____

3. Concepts/processes/procedures I have in-depth knowledge about:

   _____

   _____

   _____

4. Things I'd rather be doing:

   _____

   _____

   _____

5. Things wild horses couldn't make me do:

   _____

   _____

   _____

Skills and Talents Worksheet

Here's an opportunity to acknowledge the hidden skills and talents you possess that might be useful in your new profession. Go on, don't be shy—blow your own horn!

1. What job skills do you possess that are really outstanding? (You might want to refer to the skills inventory for inspiration.)

   _____

   _____

   _____

2. What specialized training or education do you have?

   _____

   _____

   _____

3. What do you like the most about your present job or occupation?

   _____

   _____

   _____

4. What special license(s) do you possess in your present job?

   _____

   _____

   _____

5. What have you been told that you do extremely well?

   _____

   _____

   _____

3

Consulting
Basics

As we mentioned in Chapter 1, it's possible to consult in virtually any field, both technical and nontechnical. Although the issues and problems you'll consult on will vary depending on your specialty (such as engineering, information technology, human resources, strategic planning, and so on), some aspects of running a consulting business are pretty much the same no matter what your expertise is.

▲

This chapter will cover some of the day-to-day functions involved in managing a small consulting practice, as well as strategies for providing excellent customer service.

A Day in the Life

Consultants have three basic functions: to advise clients, to implement solutions, and to teach clients how to do business better in some way. But the life of a consultant consists of much more than this. While it's likely no two days will be the same, you'll find there will be certain professional and administrative tasks you'll do on a regular basis. For instance, you'll have to prospect for clients and attend to the administrative tasks necessary to keep a small business running. On a typical day, you'll be on the phone making cold calls. You'll attend meetings of local associations and/or service groups so you can network for future business. You'll write proposals to persuade prospective clients to hire you over the competition, and later you'll negotiate contracts detailing your responsibilities. You'll also be called on to give quotes that estimate how much your services will cost for specific projects. And when you do win a contract, you'll spend time mulling over solutions to the proposed problem, then writing a comprehensive report outlining the solutions. (You'll find a sample report in Chapter 13.) Monotony is one thing you won't find in the consulting business. "And I like it that way. I like the variety," says Huntington Beach, California human resources consultant Susan Bock.

Merrily Schiavone finds herself doing a tremendous amount of e-mailing to keep her Newark, Delaware advertising consulting business running. "It's an efficient way to make contacts early in the day, especially since I'm an owl, not a lark, and I prefer to spend the afternoon and evenings doing the creative stuff," she says.

General office administration duties also will include spending time on the telephone every day fielding inquiries from interested clients and keeping up with paperwork, such as incoming mail and outgoing tax payments (since self-employed people are usually required to make quarterly estimated tax payments). You most likely will handle your own invoicing and track your receivables (although we'll discuss how an accountant can help with the financial side of your business in Chapter 5). You'll also be in charge of paying any bills incurred by the business, advertising your services, and overseeing the work of the employees you hire.

Providing Excellent Customer Service

To succeed as a consultant, you must do everything you can to set yourself apart from the competition. You want to give your clients a reason to say, "I'm really glad I chose this consultant." In other words, you want your clients to be happy at every stage of the relationship. One way to ensure that the relationship stays happy is to provide the best customer service on the planet. (For more information, read the "Now Serving" chapter in *Startup Basics*.) The best way to do this is by communicating with your client often about whether his or her expectations are being met and if the project is progressing as desired, as Bock does.

"At the end of the first month of a project, I always ask my clients whether they think value is being achieved," says Bock. "I'll give them a full refund and won't proceed any further if I determine it's not possible to deal with their unrealized expectations."

Fred Elbel, a web design and computer consultant in Lakewood, Colorado, takes a different approach to customer service: He actually gives information away free as a way to make a favorable impression. "I give a lot of free advice to customers—in fact, sometimes too much," he admits. "It could be information like how to back up a computer system. But what happens is that clients remember how I helped them, and they'll call me when they don't have the time or skill to tackle other problems." Another example of outstanding customer service comes from Stew Leonard, an entrepreneur who owns a store in Norwalk, Connecticut that's billed as "The World's Largest Dairy." Although he's not a consultant, his customer service backstory definitely is noteworthy. His store, Stew Leonard's, combines elements of Disneyland and Dale Carnegie, and it delivers a straightforward message: Have fun!

In his case, fun equals big-time profits. A few years ago, Stew Leonard was grossing more than $150 million annually, making his store the most successful supermarket in the country. Customers go out of their way to shop there, and they all agree that the reason is because it's fun. Fun is just the tip of the iceberg, however; Leonard's success rests on his scrupulous management and marketing practices, plus a devotion to customer service that borders on the fanatical. As a result, he has won the praise of Fortune 500 executives and has been cited by author Tom Peters in his book *In Praise of Excellence*.

To understand what his customers want, Leonard usually spends an hour or so each day patrolling his grocery store, which stocks around 1,000 items (compared to an average of 15,000 items found in a larger supermarket). His philosophy is simple: He gives the people only what they want—nothing more, nothing less. People who visit his store never wait in line to check out with their groceries. Leonard makes sure that each of his 29 registers is always open. And he listens to

> **Bright Idea**
> Educate yourself about the latest trends and tips in business by staying current with the latest business books on the market. The information they contain can help you do business better and help your clients do the same. News sites like BusinessWeek.com or Bloomberg.com are also great sources of current information.

his customers when they tell him something. He treats all customers who walk through his doors as if they're royalty, because in Leonard's eyes, they are.

Here's a story Leonard likes to share about a customer who came into the store during the holiday season. She was trying to return a carton of eggnog that she claimed was spoiled. Leonard told her that about 300 other customers had bought eggnog from the same batch without a problem. In short, he told her she was wrong, and she wouldn't be getting a refund.

The woman complained that she would never shop at his store again, and after she left the store Leonard realized what a mistake he had made over a 99-cent carton of eggnog. So he decided to memorialize his mistake so he would never forget it. He installed a three-ton granite boulder outside his store on which are carved the store's two cardinal rules: Rule Number 1: The Customer Is Always Right. Rule Number 2: If The Customer Is Ever Wrong, Go Back And Reread Rule Number 1.

Now, when you think about offering the best customer service possible, remember Stew Leonard. In fact, your goal should be to top his customer service philosophy—if that's even possible!

Developing a Win-Win Style

To succeed as a consultant, you need to develop a win-win style of management. This means that both you and your client must view everything you do as something positive, a means of moving forward, and/or a way to solve a problem. Your ultimate success depends on your ability to use your inner resources and strengths, as well as your ability to do whatever it takes to solve your clients' problems and challenges and to be positive and energized while you do it. When you do these things, both you and your client will come out winners.

While solving problems and addressing challenges are certainly a consultant's main functions, there's another important task consultants must undertake on the way to success, according to Melinda Patrician, a public relations consultant in Arlington, Virginia. "One thing I highly recommend," she says, "particularly to women who are consulting for organizations, is to get to know what the power structure is in that organization and get to know the support staff as well as your contact person."

That's good advice, because understanding the organization will help you make better decisions and give better advice. It also helps you to know who the go-to per-

At Your Service

Successful consultants live by these 10 credos:

1. *Accept full responsibility for your actions.* Concentrate on giving your very best, no matter how good, bad, or indifferent your client may be.
2. *Develop an attitude of optimism and positive expectations.* Begin to expect the very best from yourself, and soon others around you will see what a powerful force you present. Remember, optimists are simply people who have learned how to discipline their attitudes to their advantage.
3. *Motivate yourself to have a "never give up" style.* Make your clients feel you're there for them no matter what. In other words, go above and beyond the call of duty to fulfill your end of the agreement.
4. *Keep improving your communications skills.* When there is a breakdown in communication, chaos results. Practice your listening skills. Sometimes clients may not be clear about what they want, so ask questions so you're sure you understand what's expected of you.
5. *Believe in yourself.* When you have a high level of self-esteem, the sky's the limit.
6. *Be flexible.* Any consultant who can maintain a high degree of flexibility will gain a good reputation and have no trouble attracting new clients.
7. *Set goals.* When you have a plan of action with certain goals in mind, your goals will be easier to achieve. Remember, if you fail to plan, you plan to fail.
8. *Organize yourself.* This will impress your clients and help you become a more successful consultant.
9. *Seek more than one solution to a problem.* You also should always look for creative ways to solve those problems. Walt Disney, a true visionary if ever there was one, was a firm believer in the power of brainstorming; you should be, too!
10. *Be happy!* When you're happy, those around you will be happy, too.

son is when you need input or a decision made relating to the project you're handling. In addition, when you get to know your contact and his/her support staff, you're fostering personal relationships that are invaluable. People like to do business with people they like—and when you take the time to ask sincerely about someone's health or family or activities, you develop important ties with your clients and their support staff.

On the other hand, don't feel as though you have to be all things to all people. It's not humanly possible, and by trying to do so, you actually may be setting yourself up

▲

to fail. So before you take on a new consulting job, consider these four common mistakes fledgling consultants make in their enthusiasm and haste to land clients and make a good impression:

- *You promise more than you can deliver.* While all consultants like to think they can solve everyone's problem on time and under budget, the reality of the business is that you can't. And once you recognize that fact of the consulting life, you won't promise too much. It's very easy to listen to your client talk about the problems in their organization. The hard part comes when you sit down to solve the problems. Don't offer solutions that you're not 100 percent sure from the beginning that you can carry out.

- *You fail to be specific about the role you'll be playing.* Too often a consultant will sign a contract with a client and not have a clear understanding of what the client expects. Make sure you and your client put in writing what tasks you'll be performing and how you'll accomplish them. (You'll find some tips for creating effective contracts in Chapter 13.)

- *You fail to treat each client as an individual.* Far too many consultants rely on boilerplate reports to solve a client's problem. After all, using a report that was presented to another organization with a similar problem saves a lot of time for the consultant, since all he or she has to do is change the names, dates, and figures. But let's face it: Everyone's problems are not the same. If you want to succeed in the consulting world, you must treat all clients and their organizational challenges as unique. So while you can have a general template you use to build a report, don't use boilerplate language. That short-changes the client, and makes you look unprofessional.

> **Tip...**
>
> **Smart Tip**
> Remember that your customers are the most important aspect of your consulting business; without them, you—and your business—will never survive!

- *You may not be qualified to get the job done.* Occasionally, you may come across a client who offers you a job you know you would like to have (either for the money or for the prestige of working for that particular client), but you may not be qualified to do. Know when you should take a job and when you should turn it down. Or if you're offered a job you would never be able to do on

> **Tip...**
>
> **Smart Tip**
> Your attitude is your most priceless possession and can make the difference between success and failure as a consultant. Take time for an attitude check every day; it should always be in a positive mode.

your own, consider bringing in an associate on a temporary basis to help you. (You'll find information about hiring additional help in Chapter 7.) As a consultant, it's your job to market yourself and sell your services to clients who need your help. But at the same time, you must make sure both you and your clients are happy with the results.

Secrets of Consulting Success

Erin Blaskie, an author, motivational speaker, and internet marketing specialist, offers these suggestions for becoming a successful entrepreneur:

- *Implement ideas fast.* Don't hold back and don't dilly-dally with details and with trying to be perfect. Get ideas out there, and tweak as you go.
- *Use your strengths, and delegate the rest.* Don't try to do everything yourself. Let's face it—to be successful, you need to learn that you aren't the best person to do everything in your business. Read *The E-Myth Revisited* for a great take on what it means to wear many hats as an entrepreneur. It'll make you realize that you should focus on what you're good at and then delegate the rest. Find the right people, and they'll pay for themselves.
- *Surround yourself with a good support system.* Learn to surround yourself with positive people, and rid yourself of toxic people.
- *Do only what you love.* Don't do anything you don't love to do. Why not? You run the risk of doing a poor job or taking light-years to turn things around. We're not meant to do everything; we're meant to do the work where our passion lies and where our heart is because *that* makes us successful.
- *Work only with people who energize you.* Find clients you're inspired and energized by, who embrace your talents and who understand the way you work.
- *Limit your overhead.* Stay in the green, and you'll become more successful. Think of how much less stress you'll have when money isn't an issue!
- *Be generous.* Don't be afraid to give away information or help out your fellow businessperson for nothing in return. It feels great, and people will remember you.

4

Setting Up
Shop

Now that you have a pretty good idea of the background and skills you'll need to be a successful consultant, it's time to start laying the groundwork for establishing that business. This chapter covers tasks like setting up a home office, writing a business plan, naming your business, and addressing all those other details necessary to get your fledgling enterprise up and running.

Home Alone

One of the great things about establishing a consulting business is that your new enterprise probably won't require a large initial capital investment, particularly if you operate from your home. (Certain deed restrictions and local laws may prohibit you from doing this; check with an attorney before you proceed.)

There are many advantages to having a home office.

- *Low overhead expenses:* Work at home, and you'll avoid the high cost of commercial office space rent and utilities—which is important because you won't yet have a regular client base to help keep those bills paid.

- *Flexibility:* Do you like to work on the weekends so you can have Fridays off? Do you prefer to work vampire hours rather than a 9–5 schedule? Self-employment gives you the flexibility to set your own hours and take time off when you need it—and do it without guilt.

- *Freedom from rush hour:* In addition to steering clear of congested roads and possible road rage during peak drive time, you'll avoid wasting both time and gasoline languishing in traffic. This is a benefit many homebased entrepreneurs relish. "I've had to do an awful lot of driving in my career, so I love working at home—I wouldn't trade it for the world," says public relations consultant Bill Metten in Hockessin, Delaware.

- *Tax-deductibility:* The IRS has relaxed the rules for people who work at home, so you may be able to deduct the part of your home used for business and the related costs (like utilities). But you should check with your accountant or income tax preparer to make sure you qualify for this deduction.

Location, Location, Location

And speaking of your home office, it's recommended that, right from day one, you establish a specific place to work that's devoted strictly to business and has actual office furniture. The reasons are simple. Having an office gives you a place to go to every day where your work is done—not unlike the setup you may have had when you were working for someone else in corporate America. It also serves as a reminder that real work must be done there to support yourself and your family, something that lessens the allure of outside distractions. Finally, a dedicated space will help you draw the line between your business and home life, which is really important when you're self-employed. Especially in the early days of a new business, it can be tempting to throw yourself wholeheartedly into the business to the exclusion of your significant other, children, and personal interests. Being able to walk out of the spare bedroom that serves as your office and close the door behind you will help you to have a life—which, if you'll recall, is probably one of the reasons you decided to start your business in the first place.

"The real benefit of having an office in the basement away from the living areas is that it helps me to concentrate on the job," says Merrily Schiavone, a graphic design consultant in Newark, Delaware. "It also keeps me from running upstairs to make a bed!"

If you don't have the luxury of having a spare room that can be converted into an office, all is not lost. A corner of the living room partitioned off with a screen (available at any home décor store), a closet converted into a workstation, or even a pantry reclaimed from the canned fruit and vegetables will do. Just be sure to pick a place that's outside the mainstream of family activity, and make sure it's clear to your spouse and kids that your "special place" is for work only. You'll also want to make sure your family understands your business phone is sacrosanct and may never be answered by anyone other than you. Got a workspace in mind? You'll find more information about what it takes to equip it in Chapter 6.

Home Court Disadvantages

Although working from home gives you a lot of freedom, running a business from your home isn't all fun and games. There actually are a few disadvantages to operating from your home, including:

- *Isolation:* If you're used to working in a large office setting with plenty of people, you may experience culture shock when you first open a home-based consulting business. Make sure you develop a network of friends and other associates with whom you can huddle on a regular basis, or join a professional organization like the chamber of commerce.
- *The lure of home responsibilities:* You have to be well disciplined to work at home successfully. You must be able to say to yourself, "Self, I'm at work. I will not stop working on this proposal to do the laundry, mow the lawn, or shovel snow."
- *Constant interruptions:* Family members, friends, and neighbors may not respect your working time and space and may feel they can interrupt you any time they want. You'll have to inform them politely but firmly that your door isn't always open.
- *Lack of meeting space:* If you're like many fledgling entrepreneurs, it will be hard enough to find sufficient space for a home office, let alone a conference room. You'll probably have to make alternate arrangements when meeting with clients.

▲

Whatever you do, keep your office based at home as long as possible. "If you have broadband and telephone access there's no reason to invest in office space—yet," says Elizabeth Knuppel, a communications consultant in Durham, North Carolina. "Hold your meetings at Starbucks or meet clients for lunch or breakfast at a nice hotel until your revenue base can support the cost of a lease."

Smart Tip
Sign up for Caller ID or get an answering machine so you can screen calls during the workday. This will help you fend off unproductive social calls or annoying calls from telemarketers so you can keep your mind on business where it belongs.

Tip...

It's a Plan

The last time you went on a two-week vacation by car, did you just pack up the kids, toss a few bathing suits into the trunk, and hit the road? Probably not. As you know, it takes careful planning to get to any destination—and that goes double for when you're starting your own business. As a result, one of the very first tasks you should undertake during the startup phase of your consultancy should be the crafting of a carefully constructed business plan. Besides outlining your plans, goals, and strategies, a business plan can be helpful if you ever have to approach a lending institution for funds.

But happily, you don't have to be a writer to draw up a viable plan—you just need vision and, hopefully, a little analytical skill to help you size up your market and your competition, then create a document that addresses the opportunities. But if you do need assistance, it's readily available from sources like your local Small Business Development Center (SBDC). To find your local office, log on to sba.gov/sbdc, then go to "Tools," then "Small Business Planner." You also should check out your local bookstore or library for books or software packages that can simplify the writing process.

Basically, a business plan has seven major components:

1. *Executive summary:* In this section you'll summarize the entire business plan. Be sure to briefly describe the services you'll offer in your consultancy, mention the legal form of operation (discussed later in this chapter), and list your goals. Because you may need to seek business financing at some point, you also should mention your plans and strategies for growing the business in this section.

   The easiest way to write the executive summary is to write the rest of the business plan first, then cull the major findings from each section for inclusion in the summary. Try to keep the executive summary brief—usually 300 to 500 words is sufficient—since its purpose is to provide enough information so an interested party can get a general idea of what the report covers without reading it in its entirety.

2. *Business description:* In this section, you'll give a description of the main tasks you'll do as a consultant. Depending on the type of business you're starting, you might mention activities like analyzing clients' businesses and/or finances, troubleshooting computer problems, handling clients' public relations activities, and so on. This section is important because it identifies the scope of your responsibilities, which is important both for you and for future investors or bank officers. So be sure to give this section a lot of thought before you start writing.

   In this section, it's also important to discuss your business objectives (avoid listing "making money" as one of your objectives), project how you plan to grow the business and in what time frame, mention how many employees (if any) you'll need to operate the business, and so on. Need some help or ideas? The SBDC provides information and advice to small businesses, often at low or no charge. Entrepreneur.com also offers many suggestions for creating a viable business plan.

3. *Market strategies:* That soul-searching you did (hopefully) after reading Chapter 2 will come in handy here. In this section you'll specify exactly who will use your services, then outline a plan for reaching those prospective clients. If you found any statistics related to your target market that might be helpful, you should mention them here. Remember, too, to emphasize any characteristics that make your company unique or innovative. For example, maybe you were a media relations consultant for a Fortune 500 company for a decade. You'll want to mention that experience and the knowledge you gained during your career, as well as any significant projects and/or clients you handled, since this experience will be valuable to your prospective client base.

4. *Competitive analysis:* Create a list of potential competitors and consider what you'll do to make your business successful in the same market they serve. Start by identifying the niche market you'll cover. Do you want to service clients in a particular geographic area? Or maybe companies of a particular size? Whatever you decide, resist the urge to serve too broad a market. As a new business owner, you need to start small so you can focus your efforts effectively without getting overwhelmed.

   Next, try to identify a service your competitors don't offer so you can include it in your service mix. That's the best way to put your mark on the market and make more clients interested in using your services. For instance, a computer consultant who makes house calls for installation and repair services when the competition doesn't should instantly find him- or herself in demand by a certain segment of the computer-using public.

5. *Design and development plan:* In this section, you should outline your plans for

developing market opportunities, and set timetables for achieving them. This can be as simple as specifying that you would like to have five clients by the end of the fiscal year and outlining how you'll land and service them. Specify what resources are necessary to complete this process (money, staffing, etc.).

6. *Operations and management plan:* Using the type of information found in Chapter 3, outline the day-to-day operations of your business and provide details about the professional background and expertise of the management team (that's you). Details about operating expenses should also be included here. Chapter 12 contains a discussion of how to create an income and expense form that you can mine for information that will be suitable for your business plan.

7. *Financial factors:* Even a one-person business owner needs to know where he or she stands financially at all times, so it's important to create financial documents like an income worksheet, balance sheet, and cash flow statement. Go to entrepreneur.com for information on how to develop these forms, or work with an accountant to set them up. Then summarize this information for inclusion in your business plan.

Now, stop right where you are. Are you about to turn the page and never give another thought to constructing a business plan? If so, that's a bad move. A business plan will help to keep you on track and moving toward your goals. And don't think it has to be a document that rivals *War and Peace.* Length isn't as important as content—so put your ideas down on paper and refer to them often. It's the best way to make sure your consulting ship keeps steaming toward Port Success.

> **Tip...**
>
> **Smart Tip**
> It's important to write your first business plan yourself rather than farming it out to a business consultant, according to SCORE. That way, you learn as much as possible about your own business, which in the long run will help you understand how to make it successful.

Making It Legal

Choosing a legal form of business is another one of those decisions you should make early in the business planning process. Basically, there are four types of legal structures: sole proprietorship, partnership, corporation, and limited liability company (LLC). Here's the 411 on each. You'll find a detailed explanation of each in the "Make It Legal" chapter in *Startup Basics.*

- *Sole Proprietorship:* This is the easiest and least expensive legal structure to adopt, which is why so many startup businesses begin this way. There's little paperwork—all you do is file Schedule C, Profit or Loss from Business, when you file your personal income taxes, as well as a couple of other tax forms related to business use of your home and tax payments. Just keep in mind that the sole proprietor is also personally responsible for all of the business debt, and both personal and business assets are fair game for creditors.

- *Partnership:* Under this form, two or more people share ownership of the company, either in equal or unequal amounts, and each partner is responsible for the business debt. Profits and expenses are recorded on the partners' individual income tax forms. Partnerships work especially well for people with complementary skills, but there can be disagreements about workloads, responsibility, and other matters, so it's important to have a partnership agreement drawn up before embarking on this type of venture.

- *Corporation:* A main benefit of a corporation is that business liability against the owner(s) is limited because it's considered to be an entity separate from the owner(s). A main disadvantage of a corporation is that you have to observe certain corporate formalities, including holding an annual meeting (although it can be at Denny's rather than in a ballroom at the Hyatt), electing officers, and issuing stock certificates. It's also more expensive to form a corporation.

   There are two types of corporations. The S corp is somewhat more advantageous to a small-business owner because it's taxed like a partnership and profits/losses are reported through personal income tax forms. However, you have to qualify for S corp status. You'll gain an "Inc." designation with a C corp, as well as the requirement to fill out a lot more paperwork (because of federal, state, and local requirements). Usually you'll also pay higher taxes because both corporate earnings and personal earnings are taxed.

   "I started as a sole proprietor, but discovered some clients preferred to work with a corporation because it's better for them from a tax perspective," says Colorado market research consultant Carol Monaco. "Although a corporation does protect your personal assets, setting up a corporation is not just about protecting assets; it's about being professional."

- *Limited Liability Company (LLC):* Now available in all 50 states and the District of Columbia, the LLC combines the limited liability of a corporation and the tax benefits of a sole proprietorship or partnership. It's a good choice for a small-business owner who's leery about liability but wants to avoid the corporate formalities of a C or S corp.

> **Tip...**
>
> **Smart Tip**
> For more information about forming an LLC, review your state's laws, fees, and filing information by logging onto the Limited Liability Company Center website at limitedliabilitycompanycenter.com. The site also contains links to free downloadable documents you may need to file.

The legal form you choose will depend on your personal situation and how much risk you're willing to take. Many consultants, like Huntington Beach, California, public relations consultant Susan Bock, choose to start as a sole proprietor solely because it's the easiest type of business to form.

"I originally thought I'd work as a sole proprietorship until I had a sense of where I wanted the business to go," Bock says. "My financial planner and attorney also suggested I wait to make a choice. Eventually, I decided this was the best choice for me."

The best choice for Schiavone, the Delaware graphic design consultant, was an S corporation because of its many benefits. "Overall it's just easier for me when it comes to taxes and other matters," she says.

David McMullen, a computer consultant in Costa Mesa, California, formed an LLC after operating as a sole proprietor for the first two years. "Every quarter I've had revenue growth, and I'm now clearing quite a bit more than when I started," he says. "Back then, I didn't feel like forking out the money to become 'legal,' but since I don't want anyone coming after my personal assets, it was time to change my legal status."

With all the variables involved in selecting the most appropriate form of business for your consultancy, you'll find it helpful to talk to an attorney. The next chapter provides tips on how to pick an attorney who will meet your needs … and your budget.

The Name of the Game

What's in a name? Plenty, especially if you want your business to be successful.

When selecting a trade name for your consulting business, choose carefully. Take a few moments and browse through the local Yellow Pages, which will give you a few good lessons on what *not* to name your business.

Look under "Consultants," and you'll see a wide variety of consulting names—everything from ABC Consulting (do they teach you the alphabet?) and Kite Associates (do they teach you to make kites, or just fly them?) to The Dolphin Consulting Group (insert your favorite "Flipper" joke here). Creativity is fine, but unless your goal is to provide prospects with a good laugh or to confuse potential clients, then take some time choosing a name before hanging out your shingle for all the world to see.

Schiavone came up with the name AdHelp for her consulting business, which reflects the services she provides. "I'm actually helping people with their advertising, so I just put the words 'ad' and 'help' together," she says. "And I knew that because the name began with the letter A it would always be listed near the top [of listings]."

Riddle chose Blue Moon Communications as the name of his consulting business because he thought it was catchy and didn't limit the services he might provide in the future. It also adds a little whimsy and appealed to his sense of fun. Other entrepreneurs have found the monikers for their businesses right in front of their noses—they used variations of their names and counted on their recognition within the community.

Dr. Linda Henman, a strategy coach based in St. Louis and author of The Magnetic Boss, advises choosing a name that combines your own name and the nature of your business. "*Not* having your name as a part of your company name deprives you of an opportunity to promote your identity," she says. "On the other hand, using your name alone misses a chance to clarify the nature of your business. I think a combination is best."

As a consultant, you want to portray an aura of professionalism, so try to stay away from cutesy names for your company. If you aren't sure what to call your business, try something simple like "John Doe and Associates" or even "John Doe, Consultant." Just be sure that when you advertise in the telephone book, you're specific about the type of consulting services you offer. For example, if you offer management consulting services, make sure you're placed in that category.

Smart Tip

When deciding on a name for your consulting business, be sensitive to how that name might translate into another language. For example, if you will be dealing with non-native-speaking clients (including here in the United States), be sure your business name isn't offensive when translated into their language.

Paper Trail

Once you've selected your business name, your next step should be to register it with your local government, usually at the county level. Most states require you to file paperwork to establish your business name as a unique "assumed name," even if you're using your own name as part of the company name. Known as a dba, which is short for "doing business as," an assumed name establishes that you're the only one permitted to operate under that name in that jurisdiction. An assumed name is also necessary so you can accept and cash checks in your company name, as well as set up a business checking account (which is always recommended, no matter how small your operation may be).

The fee for a dba is nominal, usually from as little as $10 to around $60. As part of the registration process, the county will do a search of local businesses to ascertain that your name is unique. In case the name you've chosen has already been taken (which is not uncommon), be sure to have a couple of extra names in reserve.

While you're checking into that dba, you should inquire about any licenses needed to operate legally in your community. In most cases, this is a mere formality—most communities are small-business-friendly and won't object to your fledgling operation. The exception might be if your business will generate a lot of traffic that could be disruptive to your neighborhood, including employees who aren't related to you working in your home and parking their vehicles on the street. In that case, you may have to apply for a zoning variance, which is issued by your local government. Variances aren't automatically granted, so if you intend to entertain a lot of clients or hold frequent business meetings, it might be a better idea to rent office space on an as-needed basis.

A business license is also usually inexpensive—perhaps $10 or $20—and is renewable annually. Save yourself some time in line at the county courthouse by checking to see if you can apply for the license online. It's possible you'll need other state or even federal licenses to operate, depending on the kind of work you do. Check with your state licensing department for additional information.

You may find the state licensing paperwork requirements to be minimal—or nonexistent, in some states. For example, Jeffery Bartlett, a marketing research

Beware!
While you can use one of the myriad companies online to file your dba, it's always cheaper to do it yourself. For instance, a dba obtained at the county courthouse in Macomb County, Michigan, costs $10. But one online company charges $160 for the same services you can take care of yourself on your lunch hour.

Smart Tip
Business.gov, the official business link to the U.S. government, has a search tool on its site that will connect you to a listing of all the federal, state, and local permits, licenses, and registrations you'll need to run your business. Simply enter your city and state or ZIP code, and a comprehensive list with links will pop up.

Beware!
It's tempting to grab all the work that comes your way when you first start out, if only because you're worried about keeping the bills paid. But choose your work carefully—there's no point accepting jobs that don't pay enough to be worth your while, plus you'll burn out fast if you try to take on too much too soon.

consultant in Harrisburg, Pennsylvania, says there's no special license needed for the work his firm performs, which involves providing focus group facilities to clients, something that requires only a business license to operate.

In addition to a business license, if you're a consultant in a specialized field (and you know who you are), you may need a professional license to do business. Check with the appropriate state agency for additional information and clarification.

Net Worthy

The internet can be a consultant's best friend. Once you become internet savvy, you'll discover a plethora of information in cyberspace that will help you grow and expand your consulting practice. Check out these websites:

- *Association of Professional Consultants (consultapc.org):* This is an excellent resource for consultants in all fields. Members have access to publicity and promotions, professional workshops and courses, and a whole array of business information consulting professionals can use.
- *ConsultantsRegistrar.com:* This unique website contains listings of consulting firms and individuals in more than four dozen industries. With its searchable database, you'll have no trouble finding consultants you can network with in locations around the country.
- *SBA (sba.gov):* The SBA is an excellent online resource for consultants who are just starting their own practice. Everything from advice on promoting your business to financial planning is available with the click of your mouse.

Calling in the
Professionals

Now that you're on your way to establishing your consultancy, it's time to think about the experts you'll need to keep your business running. At a minimum, you'll need a trio of professionals on your team: an attorney, an accountant, and an insurance broker. While it can be hard to part with the cash for professional fees this early in the game, it's a critical move. Hiring skilled professionals will allow you to hand over work that you're probably not an expert at doing anyway while freeing you to devote all your time to the work you do best.

"If you're a true entrepreneur, this advice will go against the grain," says Dr. Linda Henman, a strategy coach in St. Louis and author of *The Magnetic Boss*. "You are self-reliant, independent, and resourceful, so why do you need help? After all, you can learn what you need to know, right? Probably, but it's a waste of time, energy, and resources, so hire experts to help so you can work in the areas in which you are the expert."

Having these pros on your management team is beneficial in yet another way. Professional advisors make your business look much more stable, solid, and professional when it comes time to approach a banker for financial assistance.

Legal Eagle

Most people think of an attorney as someone they hire to get them out of a jam. But as American banker and financier J.P. Morgan said, "I don't want a lawyer to tell me what I cannot do. I hire him to tell me how to do what I want to do." For an aspiring entrepreneur, that means having a competent ally to read the fine print of those incomprehensible contracts that no one else reads, and steer you around potential pitfalls caused by legalese. He or she also will be invaluable when you're drafting contracts of your own, if you have a contract dispute, when you're negotiating a business loan, or when you're signing a lease for a lot of money (such as when you decide to move from your home office into a commercial space). An attorney also can help you with tax issues and the process of selecting a business structure.

Colorado market research consultant Carol Monaco offers perhaps the best reason why you need an attorney: "I'm not a lawyer and I don't play one on TV, so there was no question that I needed a lawyer. In fact, I would never do business without an attorney—that would make me very nervous."

Unfortunately, a lot of startup entrepreneurs shy away from hiring the attorney they need because they think they can't afford one. This isn't necessarily the case. While it's true that the services of an attorney in a large firm might be beyond the means of a startup consultant, it's possible to find someone who can work within your financial boundaries. An attorney in a small one- or two-person practice is usually a good bet, as is someone who charges a flat fee for routine work (like writing letters or setting up a corporation) or one who offers a business startup package.

A startup package runs about $500 to $900 and usually includes the initial consultation and all activities related to the incorporation or LLC process, including the filing of paperwork with your state and other corporate formalities. Alternatively, it's possible to hire an attorney on retainer, which is paid upfront and is drawn against by the attorney as work is completed.

Attorneys typically charge $100 to $450 an hour. The amount varies depending on where you're doing business. Fortunately, there are simple ways to keep down the cost of legal fees. First, keep calls to your attorney to a minimum, since he or she is on the clock every time you call. For the same reason, be sure to have all the information and documents you need right at hand when you do call or meet. You can also ask your attorney to estimate the amount of time he or she thinks a project will take so there are no surprises later, and you should ask for an itemized statement of services to make sure you're receiving the services for which you're being billed.

While you'll find a lot of attorneys listed in the phone book, it's usually wiser to ask business colleagues or other small-business owners for a recommendation. Your local chamber of commerce or other business organizations may also be good sources of leads, as are attorney referral services, which can be found in most major metropolitan areas.

Bookmakers

Even if you've always done your own taxes and can balance your checkbook with ease, you still will need the services of a professional accountant for your business. Keeping the books can be very labor-intensive and siphons off crucial time you'll need to manage your consultancy. You'll also find it's a great relief to be able to count on someone experienced to keep your balance sheet balanced, make sure estimated tax payments are made promptly, and so on. This isn't to say, however, that you can't do the basic bookkeeping yourself using a spreadsheet program like Microsoft Excel or QuickBooks. But you'll want to engage the services of an accountant for the complicated tasks, including creating profit and loss statements, making financial projections, forecasting cash flow, setting up accounting systems, and interpreting tax law.

As with attorneys, accountants' hourly rates vary widely depending on factors such as type of practice, location, expertise, and education. For instance, the BLS says the national median hourly wage is just under $27.50, while CareerBuilder.com's website cbsalary.com, says the average hourly rate for an accountant in Concord, New Hampshire, is slightly less than the

Dollar Stretcher

Because you're not likely to have many legal fees once you've incorporated or consulted with an attorney about your legal business structure, you may find it more cost effective to purchase a prepaid legal plan. After paying a small annual fee, you'll have access to a qualified attorney for services like telephone consultations, letter writing, and contract review. You can find leads to such plans in the Yellow Pages under "Legal Service Plans."

▲

median at $25.62 per hour. On the other hand, the PCPS/TSCPA National Management of an Accounting Practice Survey says that the average hourly billing rate for accounting firm owners was $171. So obviously it pays to do some due diligence before engaging the services of a professional numbercruncher. Start the process by checking out cbsalary.com, since you can plug in your ZIP code to find out what the locals are earning.

For a referral to a reputable account-

> **Smart Tip**
> To keep your financial management fees under control, ask your accountant to help you set up basic ledgers and record keeping systems for logging data and tracking receivables. If you're computer savvy, you can easily do this yourself using a software program like QuickBooks Pro.

ant, speak to your attorney, banker, or other local small-business owners, or contact the American Institute of Certified Public Accountants branch in your state. You also can find a professional accountant on the accountant-finder.com website. When choosing an accountant, try to select someone with small-business experience, since he or she is more likely to understand your concerns and finances. You'll find additional bookkeeping strategies and techniques in Chapter 12.

Going for "Broker"

One of the more surprising things you'll discover about this business of owning your own business is the amount of insurance you should have to protect your assets and livelihood. That's why you need to establish a relationship with a capable insurance broker. A broker is usually preferable to an agent, because a broker represents many insurance products from many companies, but an insurance agent is employed by a single company and sells only that company's products. As a result, you may find that a broker can get you better policies and rates.

You can find dozens of insurance broker/agent listings in the Yellow Pages, but as with the other professionals discussed here, it's usually best to ask a business acquaintance or attorney for a referral. To find someone with that all-important small-business acumen, ask to see a client list when you're shopping around for a broker.

Once you've selected your broker, you'll want to work closely with him or

> **Smart Tip**
> Remember to keep the receipt for every item purchased for your business. Besides needing good insurance records in case of a business loss, you'll need this information at tax time, since everything from office supplies to computer equipment can be added up for a tax deduction on Form 1040, Schedule C.

her to determine exactly how much coverage you'll need. Basically, the dollar amount of coverage you'll buy will depend on the amount of risk you're willing to take; i.e., the more coverage you have, the less likely you are to be stuck making an out-of-pocket payment in the event of a business catastrophe or error.

Getting Covered

Although there's insurance available to cover just about any contingency that might occur while you're self-employed (and your agent will be more than happy to sell it to you), small-business owners like consultants generally can't afford to insure against everything that might go wrong. Nor would you want to. It's better to purchase just enough coverage to save your company from ruin in the event of a disaster (either manmade or divinely wrought). And tempting though it may be, don't skimp on important coverage. It's not worth the risk of losing everything you've built to save a few bucks.

Among the types of personal insurance consultants commonly carry are:

- *Health:* Now that you're self-employed, you'll have to shoulder this cost on your own. Fortunately, health insurance premiums are now 100 percent deductible for self-employed persons—and their employees—when they report a net profit on Schedule C, C-EZ, or F. See IRS Publication 535, Business Expenses, for more information.

- *Disability:* If you can't work due to injury or illness, this insurance will replace a percentage of your gross income. Having this type of policy can mean the difference between staying solvent and going bankrupt when you're self-employed, yet new business owners tend to forego purchasing disability insurance in the interest of saving money. Don't make that potentially devastating error.

- *Life:* This type of insurance is important for two reasons: It protects your family or significant other in case of your death, and it may be required before you can obtain a loan from a bank of other financial institution.

- *General business liability:* This is a must because it protects you (and your employees, if applicable) if you're sued when someone is hurt or accidental damage is caused on or to a client's property.

- *Equipment:* This type of policy covers damage to or loss of equipment due to fire or theft. It's a good idea for entrepreneurs who work out of their homes, especially since homeowners' insurance usually doesn't cover business equipment. Instead, a separate policy or possibly a rider is needed.

- *Property:* If you're operating out of a commercial space, you'll need property insurance to protect both the building you're working out of (if you own it) and its contents. If you're working at home, you don't need this one.

- *Business interruption:* This type of policy pays the cost of your normal business

▲

expenses if you're unable to operate due to a natural disaster (like a hurricane) or a fire, theft, or other insured loss. It may also pay for equipment losses.

- *Errors and omissions:* Imagine how you'd feel if mistakes in the work you did for a client caused him or her financial losses. Then imagine how much worse you'd feel if the client sued you. That's why you might want to consider buying this type of liability insurance.

- *Workers' compensation:* This nonnegotiable insurance is required by all 50 states and covers your employees in the event of injury or illness on the job (but not you—as the owner you don't count as an employee). The amount of coverage necessary and the percentage of salary paid to employees under workers' comp vary by state.

Because managing risk can be a complex issue and because you don't want to buy less insurance than you need, rely on your insurance broker to help you make some decisions. In the meantime, we've included an insurance planning worksheet on the next page that you can use to compare policies and premiums if you'd like to do some of the work on your own. For additional general information about the different types of insurance, refer to the "Cover Your Assets" chapter in *Startup Basics*.

Tech Troubleshooter

There's one more expert you should consider adding to your stable of business professionals: a savvy and experienced computer consultant. Unless you're a computer consultant yourself, chances are your knowledge of what makes computers go is pretty limited. That means when something goes wrong, you may not have the foggiest idea how to fix it, and you could waste valuable time trying. A computer expert can help you avoid that kind of aggravation.

"Computer problems can become a black hole," says Fred Elbel, Colorado computer consultant. "You end up spending much more time trying to fix them than you can afford. Do you want to develop your business and make money, or spend time on computer problems? It's usually better to call in an expert."

To find a knowledgeable computer pro, ask around among your friends and business associates (or even the local computer superstore employees). You'll want to find someone who makes house calls (which costs more but is worth it because you won't have to unhook your cables) and can explain in plain English what's wrong and how it can be fixed. And by the way, even if you're a computer consultant, having one on call isn't a bad idea—after all, that frees you up to consult for other people and make money.

Business Insurance Planning Worksheet

Type	Required	Annual Cost
General Business Liability		
Equipment		
Property (Casualty)		
Business Interruption		
Errors and Omissions		
Workers' Comp	Yes	
Health		
Disability		
Life		
Other		
Total Annual Costs		

6

Tools of
the Trade

One of the things that makes a consulting business such an attractive option for a fledgling entrepreneur with more ambition and enthusiasm than cash is its low startup costs. You don't have to tie up big bucks in inventory. You usually don't need employees (especially in the beginning) to keep the whole show running. You don't need a commercial office space. You may not even need an expensive professional wardrobe if you won't have a lot of face-to-face client contact.

But there are definitely some things you'll need to get the show on the road, both to make your business run more smoothly and to make sure your operation is as professional as possible. This chapter covers everything you might need to run a successful consulting business, from furniture and supplies to technology.

To estimate how much cash you'll need to get your business up and running, use the startup expenses worksheet you'll find on page 66. This worksheet lists the typical expenses you can expect to incur and has spaces where you can pencil in other projected expenses as you research your startup costs. As you do this exercise, you may find it helpful to refer to the sample startup expenses chart on page 65, which lists the expenses for two hypothetical consulting businesses: Retail Management Consulting, a sole proprietorship and low-end startup, and David Jones and Associates, a high-end startup that operates as an S corporation and has one full-time employee (the owner) and one administrative assistant.

Now here's a rundown of what you may need to launch the business.

Dollar Stretcher

Since consulting businesses generally have low startup costs, it can be tempting to sink extra cash into the high-tech computer equipment you've always wanted, or an expensive furniture-quality desk. But avoid the urge. It's always better to keep startup costs as low as possible. You can buy nicer stuff later when your cash flow is actually flowing.

Office Furniture and Equipment

A couple chapters ago, we tried to dissuade you from setting up shop on your dining room table or the ironing board in the laundry room. The reason is simple: No one can work effectively that way. Rather, you need a comfortable, user-friendly space where you can park yourself, possibly for hours on end, and where you'll have easy access to a computer, office supplies, and the other tools of your trade. Ideally, you should set up a basic office consisting of a desk or computer workstation, an ergonomic office chair, a sturdy two- or four-drawer file cabinet with drawers that extend fully, and perhaps a bookcase or two. Unless you expect to entertain clients in your home office, there's no reason why you can't keep your furniture costs down by purchasing inexpensive ready-to-assemble or even secondhand furniture in good condition. Thrift shops are an excellent source of gently used furniture, as are newspaper classifieds, online classifieds like Craigslist (craigslist.com), and auction marketplaces like eBay. (Just be sure to factor in the cost of shipping if you buy on eBay.) If you prefer new furniture, visit an office supply store such as Office Depot or Staples. They carry a wide selection of reasonably priced desks that run as little as $90 to $300 and chairs that cost $50 to $200. A computer workstation runs $80 to $200.

Personal Computer and Software

Since most consulting jobs require you to churn out consulting proposals, contracts, reports, invoices, and other documents, a reliable personal computer is a must. (News flash for anyone using an older and slower computer: This means you, too!) Fortunately, you don't have to spend a lot of money to get a really great computer. For instance, at press time Dell was offering the Inspiron 530s with a 320GB hard drive, DVD-RW drive, and a 17-inch widescreen flat-screen monitor for only $549. Add on useful extras like a laser or inkjet printer and various supplies, and a complete system may run closer to $1,000. Other useful equipment that's especially necessary for a writer, public relations consultant, or graphic arts designer includes a scanner ($100 to $200, depending on the resolution) and a portable USB flash drive (as little as $15 for a 4 GB Verbatim flash drive at OfficeMax) for storing and transporting data. Also, if you deal with art or the written word, you should consider purchasing the largest monitor you can afford, since it can help prevent eyestrain. A 19-inch Dell widescreen monitor to go with that system mentioned earlier starts at as little as $119. But that's by no means the largest monitor around. You can buy a 22-inch monitor for about $230 or less and up to a 30-inch for about $1,200—but you'll need a really big desk to accommodate them. But unless you're a techno-geek with a lot of startup funds, there's really no need to shell out that much cash on a mere monitor.

If you expect to be on the road a lot for business, a laptop computer might be a better choice than a desktop model, although laptops tend to be pricier. For example, at press time Best Buy was offering a Sony VAIO laptop with a 14-inch widescreen displayand a 250 GB hard drive, Windows 7 operating system, built-in webcam, and more for $799. A netbook is a good choice if you're interested only in a tool for accessing the internet when you're on the go. A netbook doesn't have the full capability of a laptop, but it does allow you to check your e-mail, visit social networks, and so on because it provides full access to the internet (including useful sites like Mapquest.com). A netbook is small and lightweight (about 3 pounds and just 1 inch thick), and costs around $300 or less. However, you can do many of the same things at a much lower cost with a BlackBerry or iPhone, both of which are discussed later in this chapter.

The most commonly used office productivity packages are Microsoft Office and QuickBooks Pro. Microsoft Office Professional includes Word, Excel, PowerPoint (a must for presentation mate-

> **⚠ Beware!**
> Home office expenses (like the percentage of your mortgage payment, utility bills, etc., that pertain to your business) are deductible only if you're organized as a sole proprietorship or S corporation. To take the deduction, you'll have to file Form 8829, Expenses for Business Use of Your Home, and Schedule C with your taxes.

rials), Access (for database management), Publisher, Accounting Express, and Outlook e-mail. It currently retails for $499.95, or $329.95 for the upgrade version. QuickBooks is an easy-to-use accounting package that keeps your financial records straight, manages your business checking account, and prints checks. The current edition of QuickBooks Pro 2009 retails for $199.95 (although it's possible to find it discounted for less at places like Amazon.com).

Fax Machines

With the overabundance of junk faxes that waste your paper and ink and the fax cards that are standard equipment in most computers, full-size fax machines are becoming dinosaurs. But they still come in handy to receive those important incoming messages if you don't want to leave your computer on 24/7. The good news is that fax machines are inexpensive these days—a multifunction HP Officejet machine that also scans, copies, and prints can be had for as low as $100. Be sure to check around before you buy; discount electronics stores like Best Buy usually sell these inkjet fax machines for the best prices.

Home office users often install their fax machines on their regular business phone line, but if you think you'll use your fax a lot, you may want to put it on a dedicated telephone line. It can cost from $40 to $60 to install a separate line.

Landline Phone

Telephones come in all sizes and price ranges, but avoid the impulse to cut corners on your business phone equipment. Rather, buy the best model you can afford—after all, you're likely to be on the phone a lot. A standard two-line speakerphone with auto-redial, memory dial, flashing lights, mute button, and other useful features will run $40 to $80, while a top-of-the-line model can cost $250 or more. One good source for high-quality telecommunications equipment is Hello Direct (see Appendix), which specializes in professional business telephones.

Answering Machine

With voice mail, it's a wonder anyone uses an answering machine anymore. But this old stand-by technology does have its good points, including the fact that you can tell at a glance whether you have a message waiting. A stand-alone digital answering machine costs as little as $15–$30; a cordless phone/answering machine combo runs from $35–$180.

Cell Phone

A cell phone is an absolute must for a consultant, especially if you'll be out of your office a lot or if you manage on-site projects.

Home Away from Home

If you can't work out of your home, but you also can't afford to lease traditional office space at the genesis of your business, consider an office-sharing arrangement instead. For a monthly fee, you can rent a fully furnished private space (usually 500 square feet or less) in the office building in the neighborhood of your choice. Such rentals often come with everything you need to make a good impression on a prospect or client, including a reception area with a receptionist, a telephone answering service, a conference room, and a genuine business address for mail and package deliveries. For an extra fee, you may be able to obtain administrative support, photocopying, videoconferencing, and other useful business services.

If you don't need space on an ongoing basis, you may be able to rent space on a per-use basis from an office-sharing company. Under this arrangement, you rent an office space for just a few hours or a day here and there on a first-come, first-served basis. You can find office-sharing companies in the Yellow Pages under Office and Desk Space Rental Service.

As you no doubt know, today's wireless plans are very affordable and include hundreds of minutes of calling time, text messaging, and other useful features. Camera phones are also handy for sending photos of job sites, products, and other details to your clients, especially if you prefer not to carry a digital camera with you.

Since your usage level will probably be high, look for a plan that includes a large number of monthly minutes and free weekend calling. For example, one deal offered by a big-name cellular provider includes 450 minutes of anytime nationwide calling time, unlimited nights and weekends, and unlimited calling to its 8 million wireless customers for $40. If you need a phone, be sure to check out the plans that provide a free phone with service activation. One such company is Verizon, which at press time had a $60 monthly plan that included a free Samsung Gleam phone and a Plantronics Explorer 232 Bluetooth headset with a two-year contract. If that's not cool (or feature-enabled) enough for you, there's a plethora of other phones to choose from, including the BlackBerry and iPhone (both discussed below), which can run up to $400 or more. See "Services" on page 60 for a more complete rundown of monthly service charges.

BlackBerry and iPhone

Voice communication tools are fine, but everyone knows that having internet access, instant messaging (IM), and text messaging capabilities right in your pocket no matter where you roam can really help you do business better. So you may find that a full-featured phone like a BlackBerry or an iPhone is a necessity. A BlackBerry smartphone is a combination e-mail, Bluetooth-enabled cell phone, wireless internet, IM, and GPS device. You also can purchase additional applications (apps) right from your phone for everything from organizational tools to games. The BlackBerry Pearl starts as low as $99, while a high-end RIM BlackBerry Bold is more than $659.

The iPhone also offers more features than an ordinary phone, although in the corporate world it's considered to be more of a multimedia entertainment device than a business tool (its widescreen iPod is one reason why). According to reviewers in the know, iPhone apps (25,000 of them and counting) are much more advanced and nimble than BlackBerry apps, but the device's QWERTY keyboard isn't as user-friendly. A 3G iPhone starts at $199.

Toll-Free Numbers

Twenty-five years ago, only large corporations were able to afford toll-free telephone numbers. But advances in technology have made it possible for nearly every business to have a toll-free number, no matter what its size.

John Riddle, the Bear, Delaware fundraising and editorial consultant, believes that, depending on who your target market is, a toll-free number can be the deciding factor in whether your consulting business succeeds. He certainly has used a toll-free number to great advantage. When he was selling ad space in his fundraising newsletters, he discovered that his toll-free number was his secret weapon.

"Many times I asked advertisers why they selected my newsletter to advertise in, and more often than not, their reply was, 'Because you had a toll-free telephone number,'" Riddle says. "It was my only advantage over the competition."

Copy Machine

While not an absolute necessity, a copy machine can be a convenient addition to your home office. A basic desktop model costs as little as $180, but a digital model like the Xerox C123, which kicks out up to 23 copies per minute at 600 dpi, sends faxes, and prints documents, starts at about $3,500.

Keep in mind, however, that if you need to do a big copying job, especially one that requires collated, stapled, double-sided copies, your best bet is to take it somewhere like FedEx Office. Your time is better spent consulting than copying.

Supplies you'll need for your copier include copy paper and toner cartridges, both of which are readily available from your local office supply store. A case of copy paper (10 reams) runs about $35 to $70, and a toner cartridge for a personal copier (which yields about 2,000 copies) is around $100. A digital copier toner cartridge (like for the Xerox copier mentioned earlier) sells for about $125 and makes up to 30,000 copies.

Postage

If you expect to do large or frequent mailings either for yourself or your clients, you should consider investing in a postage meter. You'll pay at least $20 a month to lease a standard postage meter, and then you'll pay for postage as you go, either online at usps.com or at the post office. To qualify for bulk mailing discounts, you'll also need a permit, which is free, but you'll have to pay an annual bulk mailing fee at every post office where you enter and pay for your mail. For more information, go to usps.com and search for "Business Mail 101." Alternatively, you can rent a small-business postage meter and scale kit like the one sold by Pitney Bowes (pitney-works.com). The cost to rent this type of equipment starts at $20 monthly; you must also ante up for the cost of postage and supplies, such as ink and mailing labels.

You should also have a postage scale to make sure you're affixing enough postage to your outgoing mail. A digital scale runs $40 to $70 for a model that can handle a 10-pound load.

Tip...

Smart Tip

It's not possible to own a postage meter outright; only the USPS and its authorized meter manufacturers can own them. But they'll be happy to lease you one as long as you keep those monthly payments coming. For more information on postage meter leasing, check out "Business Mail 101" on the USPS site at usps.com.

Office Supplies

You probably can launch your business using whatever pens, paper, sticky notes, and other office supplies you already have on hand around the house. If you're short on supplies, you should budget about $30 to get yourself started. And here's a time-saving tip: The larger office supply chain stores usually will deliver your order of $50 or more directly to your doorstep in about 24 hours and at no extra charge.

You'll also need a supply of business cards, letterhead, envelopes, and brochures. A quick print shop like Sir Speedy or an online printing company like ColorPrintingCentral.com can design and produce these items for you. (We've listed a few companies in the Appendix that you can check out.) To get the most competitive quote, try using an online source like Print Quote USA (printquoteusa.com). All you do is type in the specs for your job, and the website will do the rest. An informal price survey revealed that 1,000 full-color 8½-by-11-inch brochures printed on good-quality paper start at around $185. Business cards start at around $35 for 1,000 one-color business cards from an office supply superstore like Office Depot, while a box of 250 sheets of one-color custom-printed letterhead on good quality stock costs as little as $75. A box of matching custom-printed envelopes costs about $55.

Services

Now that you've estimated the cost of all the equipment you're likely to need, here's a rundown on what it should cost to make everything operate in tandem:

> **Beware!**
> While it can be tempting to use prepackaged office store stationery to print your own letterhead and business cards, don't do it. Although you'll save money by printing these materials on the cheap, the finished product won't project the kind of professional image you need to inspire confidence in your new clients.

- *Phone and fax:* These expenses run approximately $33 per line per month, as well as about $2 extra for voice mail if it's not part of a monthly service plan. You also should have call waiting, call forwarding, and caller ID, so check with your regional phone company to find out what types of money-saving packages it offers. These bundled packages often include long-distance minutes as well, which makes them a great value.

- *Cell phone:* Typical packages that include voice mail and other standard features run anywhere from $40 to $80 per month and include 400 or more minutes of peak calling time.

    If you prefer not to commit to a multiyear contract when you sign up, you can expect to pay an activation fee of about $30.

- *Toll-free numbers:* All the major telecom companies offer toll-free service at reasonable rates. For example, AT&T charges $15 per month and as little as 5.9 cents per minute for state-to-state and regional long distance, plus it's possible to have your toll-free calls ring on your cell phone. You'll find contact information for several telecom companies that offer toll-free service in the Appendix.

- *Internet:* There are many options when it comes to internet service. Basically, there are five ways to connect. A dial-up connection through an ISP is the least expensive at as little as $10 per month, but it's also the slowest of the options. A DSL line is faster and will cost about $30 to $40 per month for basic service. Broadband, which is offered through your local cable TV company, is lightning-fast and fairly reasonable at about $40 a month on top of your regular cable TV bill. Finally, if you're ready to dump your terrestrial connection, Broadband high-speed satellite internet service is an option if you're in an area that doesn't offer cable broadband or DSL (especially if you're in a rural area). This type of service and installation is no longer a budget breaker, since prices have dropped dramatically in the past few years. For example, SkyWay USA (skywayusa.com) now offers entry-level service at $30 a month for 256 kbps, or up to $80 for 1.5Mbps. With this plan, you'll need a big honking 30-inch satellite dish ($149 before $100 mail-in rebate), which costs $50 to ship by FedEx Ground. You'll also pay $150 for professional installation, if needed (although you can get a free self-installation kit), and a $25 service activation fee.

Vehicle

Even if your consulting practice keeps you in your home office most of the time, eventually you'll have to hit the road to meet with prospects, oversee projects or events, or schmooze with clients over lunch. For this reason, a well-maintained vehicle is a must. The good news is that you can depreciate the cost of your vehicle when you file your business tax forms. The bad news is, only the percentage of the vehicle that's actually used for business can be depreciated. So if you're also using your car or other vehicle for family transportation or other per-

sonal use, you'll have to keep careful written mileage records. Additionally, in 2009 those business miles were deductible at a cost of 55 cents per mile, so that mileage log is important. For guidance on depreciation, check out IRS Publication 946, How to Depreciate Property; and Publication 463, Travel, Entertainment, Gift & Car Expenses, which can be downloaded from the IRS website at irs.gov.

While you don't have to drive a dark-colored, conservative sedan to make a good impression, keep in mind that many

▲

family vehicles (like the family minivan with Cheerios strewn around the back seat, or a mud-splashed pickup) may not send the message that you're a serious consultant who can be trusted with your clients' important work (and consulting dollars). If you can't afford to buy or lease a new vehicle, at least keep the one you own clean, both inside and out, at all times.

The Bottom Line

If you've been entering your estimated costs on the startup expenses worksheet on page 66, you'll have a pretty accurate idea of how much capital it will take to launch your new consulting business. It's likely the costs will be modest and you'll be able to finance that startup with personal savings, the way both Susan Bock of Huntington Beach, California and Merrily Schiavone of Newark, Delaware did. But if you think you're going to need a little financial help, it's not too soon to start the financing crusade. See Chapter 13 for additional tips on how to obtain financing.

Sample Office Equipment and Supplies Expenses

	Retail Management Consultants	David Jones & Associates
Office Equipment		
Computer/Printer	$550	$1,100
Software		
Microsoft Office	$500	$500
Intuit QuickBooks	$200	
Surge Protector	$10	$20
Multipurpose Fax/Scanner/Copier	$100	
Copy Machine	$180	
Digital Postage Scale	$40	$40
Phone	$90	$150
Cell Phone	$40	$100
Answering Machine	$25	
Office Furniture		
Desk	$80	$300
Chair	$50	$400
File Cabinet(s)	$40	$80
Bookcase(s)	$70	$140
Office Supplies		
Business Cards	$35	$35
Brochures	$185	$185
Letterhead, Envelopes	$130	$130
Miscellaneous Supplies (pens, folders, etc.)	$30	$50
Printing/Copier Paper	$35	$35
Extra Printer Cartridges	$30	$85
Extra Fax Cartridges	$25	
Copier Toner	$100	
CD-RW Discs	$15	$15
Mouse Pad	$10	$10
Total	**$1,965**	**$3,980**

Office Equipment and Supplies Worksheet

	Estimated Costs
Office Equipment	
Computer/Printer	
Software	
Microsoft Office	
Intuit QuickBooks	
Surge Protector	
Multipurpose Fax/Scanner/Copier	
Copy Machine	
Digital Postage Scale	
Phone	
Cell Phone	
Answering Machine	
Office Furniture	
Desk	
Chair	
File Cabinet(s)	
Bookcase(s)	
Office Supplies	
Business Cards	
Brochures	
Letterhead, Envelopes	
Miscellaneous Supplies (pens, folders, etc.)	
Printing/Copier Paper	
Extra Printer Cartridges	
Extra Fax Cartridges	
Copier Toner	
CD-RW Discs	
Mouse Pad	
Total	

Sample Startup Expenses

Item	Retail Management Consultants	David Jones & Associates
Office Equipment, Furniture, Supplies	$1,965	$3,980
Business Licenses	$30	$30
Phone (line installation charge)	$40	$80
Employee Wages and Benefits (first six months)	$2,500	
Startup Advertising	$250	$500
Legal Services	$200	$900
Insurance (annual cost)	$1,500	$2,500
Membership Dues	$300	$500
Publications (annual subscriptions)	$60	$300
Online Services (broadband)	$40	$40
Website Design	$1,000	$3,500
Web Hosting, Domain Name (annual cost)	$60	$60
Subtotal	$5,445	$14,890
Miscellaneous Expenses (roughly 10% of total)	$545	$1,500
Total	**$5,990**	**$16,390**

Startup Expenses Worksheet

Item	Estimated Cost
Office Equipment, Furniture, Supplies	
Business Licenses	
Phone (line installation charge)	
Employee Wages and Benefits (first six months)	
Startup Advertising	
Legal Services	
Insurance (annual cost)	
Membership Dues	
Publications (annual subscriptions)	
Online Services (broadband)	
Website Design	
Web Hosting, Domain Name (annual cost)	
Subtotal	
Miscellaneous Expenses (roughly 10% of total)	
Total	

7

Help Wanted

When you first open the doors to your consulting practice, you may be able to handle all the operations by yourself. But as your business grows, you may need help handling administrative details or completing the actual consulting assignments. So as painful as it might be (from a financial standpoint, at least), it might be time to bring in some help. Think of it this way: Do you really have the time to stuff

1,000 brochures into envelopes and affix mailing labels and postage? Can you afford to spend time filing proposals or updating your prospect list when you could be using that time more effectively marketing your services—and signing up new clients? If not, then you'll need to bring some help onboard.

There are many benefits to farming out some of your day-to-day responsibilities:

- *You save time and money better spent on consulting work.* By having someone concentrate on the more routine office tasks (opening the mail, filing, answering phones, etc.), you can focus all your efforts on recruiting new clients. After all, would you really want to lose a $500-per-day client because you were too frugal to hire someone to take those brochures mentioned earlier to the post office, or run to the office supply store for legal pads?

- *You don't have to worry about being away from the office.* If you're a one-person operation, it's hard to be on the road marketing your services if you're worried about clients getting your voice mail. And while you certainly can field those calls by carrying your cell phone with you wherever you go, the files or other information you need might be back in your home office. You'll seem more responsive to clients' needs if you can have your assistant respond immediately to requests, even when you're away.

- *You have someone who can offer feedback.* If you're an extrovert or someone who thrives on social interaction, you might find it pretty lonely to work by yourself all day, every day. The right employee can provide the human interaction you need, while offering another perspective, providing feedback, and proposing new ideas, all of which can be energizing and stimulating.

A Helping Hand

Since keeping your operating expenses low when you first begin a new business is always advisable, you probably shouldn't put a regular employee on your payroll in the startup phase. Instead, consider using a virtual assistant service for your temporary administrative needs. Such services are easy to find in the Yellow Pages or by searching on WhitePages.com. Rates for administrative tasks depend on a variety of factors, including how large or small the virtual assistant service is and what types of services it provides. But don't select a virtual assistant service just because it happens to have the lowest prices in town. Instead, ask for references, preferably from other consultants who have used its services, as well as other small-business owners.

A person from a virtual assistant service doesn't work directly for you; usually he or she is an employee of or an independent contractor working for that service. Today, such administrative people most likely will work off site in their own home office. If you do need someone to work on site with you, you should be able to arrange that, too, but this is likely to result in additional fees.

Temp Talk

There are several advantages to hiring temporary employees to help out when you're in a crunch.

- *You can have temporary workers for as long as you want them.* They are available to work by the day, week, or month, and you set the start and end dates to suit your project and budget.
- *You can avoid the headaches involved in the hiring process.* Just pick up the telephone, call the employment agency, and everything will be taken care of for you.
- *You don't have to worry about employee-related expenses, such as taxes, Social Security, and workers' comp.* The temp agency pays them.
- *You pay only for the hours they work.* Vacation time, personal days, and sick time are all the responsibility of the temporary agency.

Another viable option is to bring in a temporary employee. While this option is somewhat pricey, this is sometimes the best solution, especially if your consulting business is seasonal. In addition, when you hire a temp, you don't have to worry about laying someone off when business slows down, plus the next time you need help, you'll have an experienced person you can call on.

Another type of employee who should be mentioned here is the independent contractor (aka freelancer or—yes!—consultant). This is a person who also is not on your payroll, but represents you and handles your work as though it's his or her own. In exchange, you pay the freelancer either an hourly wage or a salary. You're not obligated to offer benefits, nor do you pay employment taxes, withhold FICA and other taxes, or pony up for workers' compensation insurance.

If you go this route, beware that the IRS has strict definitions about the difference between an employee and an independent contractor. To make sure you don't incur any penalties due to misclassifying your freelancer, visit irs.gov and type "independent contractor vs employees" in the search window. You should also pick up a copy of Publication 15-A, Employer's Supplemental Tax Guide, from your nearest IRS field office. You can also download it from the IRS website.

The Hiring Process

Temporary employees and independent contractors can be a big help, but the day will come when you'll need to hire someone on a permanent basis. Basically, you need a perfect employee who shows up for work early, works hard, stays late, and doesn't worry about overtime or comp time, right? Wrong. To begin with, there's no such thing as a perfect employee. And that's OK, because a perfect person would probably drive you nuts anyway. What's important is that you find the right person for the job, and the way to do that is screen prospects carefully, then choose wisely.

The first step toward finding the right person for your business is to draft an accurate job description that covers all the duties your new employee will handle. When creating the job description, be sure to:

- *Decide how many hours a week your new employee will work.* You may find that at least in the beginning of your venture into employee management, a part-time employee (20 to 30 hours a week) will be sufficient. If you're really busy, you may need a full-timer (35 to 40 hours a week) right out of the box.

- *Specify the job title.* Titles may not seem important to you, but to some employees, a title is worth as much as the money they're getting paid. For example, consider the title "administrative assistant" vs. "administrative associate." Even if the pay and the duties are the same, the "associate" title gives the employee a feeling of importance and ownership.

- *Outline the specific responsibilities the employee will handle.* If you don't include everything upfront, you may run into trouble down the road.

- *Specify the educational experience required for the job.*

- *Define additional work-related experience required.*

- *Specify to whom the employee will report.*

- *List special physical requirements, if any.* For example, if your office regularly receives boxes of books that weigh more than 40 pounds each, indicate that the employee must have the physical strength to lift them.

> **Tip...**
>
> **Beware!**
> It's usually not a good idea to dive into your pool of friends and relatives for potential employees. If you hire them and they don't work out for some reason, you not only lose an employee—you also lose a friend or you alienate family members.

Screening Applicants

Once you place an ad or let friends and business associates know you have an opening, the resumes should start arriving right away. Although an impressive resume may lead you to believe that a candidate is definitely the one you want to hire, be cautious. It's easy for job applicants to make themselves look better than they really are through well-crafted resumes. This isn't to say that most people lie on their resumes (although there has been an increase in resume-related fraud over the past decade), but as the employer, you need to take claims made on paper with a hefty grain of salt. Because your time as a consultant is valuable, you need to weed out those people who aren't qualified by checking references once you've narrowed down the field. If you find applicants who are impressive on paper, give them a call and talk with them for a few minutes. Screening job applicants by phone will save you wasted hours in the long run. Before you make that telephone call, jot down a few notes and questions you should be prepared to ask, including:

- Why do you want the job?
- Why are you qualified to take the job?
- What's your best quality?
- What are your weaknesses?

If after asking those four questions, you still feel the person may be a good candidate for your consulting business, make an appointment for an in-person interview.

For more information on job descriptions and screening, interviewing and hiring candidates, read the "Staff Smarts" chapter in *Startup Basics*.

> **Tip...**
>
> **Smart Tip**
> Check with your local library and bookstore for publications that show you how to write the perfect job description. One to check out: *The Job Description Handbook* by Margaret Mader-Clark (Nolo Press), an all-in-one resource for companies of all sizes.

Partnering for Success

Having a business partner is similar to having a spouse. In a marriage, you and your partner need to agree on everything, never have any fights about money, and have the same dreams and goals. Since a marriage can never be that perfect, it's not realistic to expect to find the perfect business partner, either.

Nevertheless, a partnership can be a wonderful thing if the partners have complementary skills, have similar business goals, and are reasonable and willing to negotiate when it comes to job responsibilities and tasks. It also helps if both partners have similar working habits. For example, if one person is committed to working until the job gets done when it's crunch time on a big project, but the other prefers to hold "business meetings" during happy hour at Buffalo Wild Wings, the friction that will result can torpedo a partnership pretty fast—and that can be detrimental or even fatal to the business relationships you've forged with clients. Finally, it really helps if both partners genuinely like each other. You don't have to be godparents for each other's kids or pal around outside the office, but the business relationship definitely will be stronger and more harmonious if you enjoy each other's company, laugh at each other's jokes, and really want each other to succeed.

To forge a strong relationship, be sure to draw up a written partnership agreement that spells out each partner's responsibilities and rights in detail, as well as what happens if one partner leaves the company. This document becomes part of the partnership agreement and is the legal muscle you need to make sure each partner lives up to his or her part of the deal, especially if there ever are any minor (or major) misunderstandings about each partner's role. Additionally, if you don't have such an agreement and an argument occurs, the laws that govern your state will take precedence when settling a dispute—and you definitely don't want that to happen.

Also, it's crucial to have a partnership agreement if you and your business associate will not be full partners in the venture. Say, for instance, you'll have the major responsibility for the business, but there's a fair amount of work you're not entirely qualified and/or interested in doing. So you might bring on a partner with a 30 percent stake in the business. Or perhaps one of the partners is a silent partner whose checkbook does more talking than he or she does when it comes to business matters. Either way, your partnership agreement needs to state exactly how many shares in the business each partner owns, as well as how the business will handle the departure of one of the partners, both in terms of finances and workload.

In a perfect world, you'll pick the right partner, have the same goals and work ethic, and work together enthusiastically to turn your fledgling business into a huge moneymaker. But if you're concerned about getting all those things right, you might find it's better to hire an associate consultant instead who will work under your direction, rather than as a business partner. Just make sure you have a noncompete clause in your contract with your associate so if she or he leaves your organization, they will be prohibited from starting a similar consulting business for a specific period of time. (The standard time period is 18 months.)

The Careers in Consulting website at careers-in-business.com says that the pay range for an associate without a bachelor's degree is $25,000 to $60,000, with compensation related to the size of the firm and the geographical area in which it operates. A bachelor's degree drives the range up to $40,000–80,000. Both salaries may be too rich for your blood when you start your new business (in fact, you'll probably be ecstatic to earn that much yourself in the early years). However, if you can swing the salary, good places to find an associate are professional associations, industry newsletters, and colleges and universities. Look for enthusiasm, critical thinking, and time management skills, and make sure the candidate is a fast learner.

> **Beware!**
> While you never want to start a partnership thinking that one day your partner could decide to pull out, set up shop for themselves, and literally put you out of business, the reality is, it could happen. An ironclad partnership agreement with a noncompete clause can put these fears to rest.

Anteing Up

Although it's not necessary to divulge to your candidates how much a job pays at the first interview, it's definitely something you need to decide before you call in the reinforcements. Obviously, if you're hiring someone who will have a great deal of responsibility, like an associate who has almost as much responsibility as you do, he or she should be paid more than the person hired to open the mail and answer your phone. By the same token, a full-time associate who has a higher level of responsibility should probably be hired as a salaried rather than an hourly employee—not so you can milk that person for a lot of overtime without pay, but because that's the more professional way of paying a valued employee.

Coming up with an equitable pay scale can be tricky. According to the BLS (bls.gov), management analysts who consult in the management, scientific, and technical fields earned a median hourly wage of $35.37 in 2008, or $73,570 per year, or an hourly mean wage of $46.35, or $96,420 per year. Secretaries (except those working in the legal, medical, and executive fields) earned $13.96, while office clerks earned $12.17. Obviously, these hourly wages far exceed the U.S. minimum wage, but you probably won't want to pay on the low end of the scale, even for the humblest employee. Shoot for a wage somewhere in between the median wages discussed above and the current minimum wage. You can find a list of minimum wages by state on the U.S. Department of Labor's website at dol.gov/esa/minwage/america.htm.

Don't want to try to guess what's fair? Then consider calling one of the consultant organizations listed in the Appendix and ask what the average wage is. Chances are, they've done surveys and would have that data at hand for specific industries. Alternatively, you could ask other consultants with whom you're friendly what they're paying their staff. Most people will be happy to share this kind of information. (Just don't ask them to divulge client names.) Finally, try a website like CareerBuilder.com (cbsalary.com), where you can find out the average salaries in your area for a wide range of careers.

Fringe Benefits

If you're really going to do this employee thing right, you also need to consider offering benefits to your new staffer(s). A good benefits package is not only a powerful draw for new hires, but is also a great retention tool. Of course, there's no denying that benefits can be expensive. A recent survey by the U.S. Department of Labor's Bureau of Labor Statistics indicated that the average cost of benefits per hour is 29.2 percent, which can be prohibitive for a small-business owner. Your cost is more likely to be around 8 to 10 percent, because you'll probably offer just the basics. But you'll find that offering even basic medical insurance and other benefits can help to attract better, more qualified employees.

Benefits typically offered by entrepreneurs in professional fields include:

- Group health and life insurance
- Vacation and holiday pay
- Sick pay
- Flexible hours

Other highly desirable benefits include pension plans, profit sharing plans, and Simplified Employee Pension plans. But don't worry about those particular benefits for now. You're not likely to

Smart Tip

Hiring another consultant as a subcontractor can be a great way to augment or expand the services you offer. Subcontractors can bring specialized skills to the table, which allows you to take on work that you may otherwise not be able to complete yourself.

offer this level of perks early in your consulting career, and, frankly, just offering health insurance can be a big enough draw for employees. For more information on offering employee benefits, check out the "Perk Up" chapter in *Startup Basics*.

Taxes

No discussion of employees would be complete without addressing the issue of payroll taxes. Employers (even those with only one employee) must withhold several kinds of taxes from employees, including income tax, FICA (aka Social Security),

Beware!

If you decide to take on a partner, make sure that any checks you write require both of your signatures. This will prevent any surprises when it comes to the financial end of your business.

and Medicare. It's also necessary to keep detailed records about the amounts withheld and when the funds are sent to the IRS (usually on a quarterly basis). For more information about withholding and taxes, pick up a copy of the IRS Publication 15, Employer's Tax Guide, as well as Publication 583, Starting a Business and Keeping Records. Both are available online from irs.gov or at your local IRS office.

Those are just the payroll taxes. As an employer, you also must pay:

- The matching portion of the FICA, or Social Security, tax, which in 2009 was 6.2 percent
- The matching portion of Medicare taxes (1.45 percent)
- State unemployment tax (the amount varies by state)
- Self-employment tax on your own

Dollar Stretcher

Check with your local community college to see if there are any student interns who would be able to spend time in your office for a few hours each week. That way you get free or low-cost help, and the student gets valuable hands-on professional experience.

earnings (which is the Social Security tax on your personal earnings since you're self-employed; 13.9 percent in 2009)

- Federal Unemployment Tax, which pays for unemployment insurance programs (in 2009, another 6.2 percent on the first $7,000 in wages, or just 0.8 percent if you pay state unemployment insurance)
- Workers' compensation insurance (the amount varies by state)

It's almost enough to make you want to do it all alone, isn't it? But look on the bright side: If you're using a minimum-wage staffer, the taxes don't amount to a lot, and you can recoup the cost by building extra fees into client contracts.

Bright Idea

It can be hard to keep up with all the changes in employer tax reporting and rates. But the IRS will gladly help. It offers eight publications (including the ones mentioned in this chapter) that cover everything you need to know. For a complete list, go to the Social Security Administration website at ssa.gov/OP_Home/handbook, then search for "1413 handbook."

Back to
School

As you know, one of a consultant's greatest strengths is his or her knowledge of a particular industry or business. As a result, keeping abreast of changes and innovations in your field is a must if you want to be an effective advisor. One way to do this is by taking classes to update your knowledge, reading publications pertinent to your field, and joining industry-related organizations. Read on

▲

for information about the consulting organizations, publications, and certification programs that can help you stay informed and ultimately do business better. You'll find contact information for each resource discussed here, as well as others, in the Appendix.

Industry Associations

No matter which type of consultancy you're starting, from information technology to turf grass management, there's probably an association devoted exclusively to it. Space constraints don't allow us to delve into a discussion of all those specialized organizations here, so instead, here's a look at some of the broadbased organizations you may find helpful as you embark on your consulting career.

- *Association for Consulting Expertise:* Based in Maine, this organization promotes the growth of members as well as public awareness of the capabilities of today's consultants. It offers a referral service, networking opportunities, discounts on memberships and merchandise, and more. The annual dues are $125.

- *Association of Professional Communication Consultants (APCC):* OK, so this is one of the more specialized organizations. But communications consulting is such a prominent field that we're including the organization here. APCC offers a wide range of benefits and resources, including promotional and marketing opportunities, tele-seminars, e-mail discussion forums, business tools like sample proposals and contracts, and more. The annual membership fee is $50.

- *Association of Professional Consultants (APC):* Established in 1979 to provide businesses with a resource for locating qualified consultant services, APC focuses on marketing and business practice development through referrals, networking opportunities, marketing and practice management programs, and support teams. It also offers a speakers directory and discounts on APC business functions. Dues are $200 annually, with a one-time $75 processing fee when you join.

- *Canadian Association of Management Consultants (CAMC):* For our friends to the north, CAMC offers professional development opportunities such as online courses, local workshops and seminars, networking opportunities, a certification program, insurance programs, and more. Dues are approximately $590 annually.

- *Professional and Technical Consultants Association (PATCA):* The wide-ranging membership of this organization includes independent consultants and principals in small firms in fields ranging from hardware and software engineering to human resources, marketing, management, and other technical and nontechnical fields.

  Three verifiable professional references are required with your membership application, and the annual dues for an associate membership (the category designed for consultants with less than one year of full-time consulting experience) are $395. Benefits include monthly networking meetings, professional development seminars, access to the members-only knowledge library, legislative updates, and more.

- *TechServe Alliance (formerly National Association of Computer Consultant Businesses):* We've decided to include this specialty organization on the list because IT consultants are in such high demand. This group offers business tools, including model business contracts, white papers, networking resources, education, health insurance and retirement planning, and its official publication, *Monitor Online*. Annual dues are $1,200 for businesses with revenues under $2 million, with a one-time initiation fee of $500.

One more organization bears mentioning. The Institute of Management Consultants USA offers many resources for members, including an annual conference, a certification program, blogs and RSS feeds, and more. However, you must have at least five years of full-time consulting experience and a bachelor's degree to be eligible for membership, which costs $295 per year with a $50 application fee. Since access to the blogs and feeds is free, you might want to tune in there until you earn your consulting "wings."

Publications and E-zines

Another way to stay current on news, information, events, and trends in the consulting field is by subscribing to industry publications. Some you might consider include:

- *Consultants News:* Geared toward larger consulting firms, this newsletter nonetheless provides interesting reading even for fledgling consultants. A subscription (26 print and online issues) is $349 a year, and the subscription includes online archive access and e-mail alerts. You can try a free issue by going to the Kennedy Consulting Research & Advisory website at kennedyinfo.com.

- *Consulting Magazine:* Sent free of charge to senior-level consultants making the really big bucks (as in seven figures), but you can subscribe for $99 a year until you hit that benchmark. Available in both print and digital form, the magazine covers events, thought leadership, industry intelligence, lifestyle issues, and more. Published bi-monthly by Kennedy Information. Subscribe (or see if you qualify for that free subscription) at consultingmag.com.

Dollar Stretcher

You can deduct the cost of professional publications on your business income taxes. Be sure to retain a copy of your canceled check or an invoice paid in full with your tax records as proof of payment.

- *Kennedy Consulting Research & Advisory:* A free e-newsletter from Kennedy Information Inc. with commentary on news concerning the consulting industry. Subscribe at kennedyinfo.com/consulting/periodicals/kennedywire.

- *Management Consulting News:* A monthly newsletter and website for management consultants that's published on the first Tuesday of the month. Current and past issues are available at no charge at managementconsultingnews.com.

Bright Idea
In addition to subscribing to publications relevant to your area of expertise, you need to be a regular reader of publications like *The Wall Street Journal, Fortune,* and *BusinessWeek.* They'll keep you abreast of changes and trends in the business world that can impact your consultancy.

Certification

Certification from a recognized consulting organization can enhance your reputation and increase your credibility, although in most cases, you must be a practicing consultant for a period of several years (usually five) before you can become certified. You can earn certifications from the Canadian Association of Management Consultants and the Institute of Management Consultants, both of which are discussed above.

For Further Study

If you prefer to take a more academic approach in your learning, you may be able to start or continue your professional development at the university level. Some universities offer certificates in consultancy through their extended learning or continuing education departments. Among them are American Century University, which offers a management consulting program through its graduate school (centuryuniversity.edu) and Hawai'i Pacific University (hpu.edu). You might try contacting your local university or community college to find out if they offer similar programs.

Bright Idea
Pursuing a general business education (or an MBA if you already hold an undergraduate degree) can really give you an edge in your profession. Coursework in marketing, public relations, organizational change, and finance can be particularly useful.

You don't have to spend big bucks to improve your skills as a consultant/business owner. As mentioned earlier, many professional and service organizations offer seminars in various topics of interest to their members, so it pays to keep an eye on their special event calendars to catch their free or low-cost workshops.

SCORE!

Imagine a resource that helps you build your business, provides current resources, and connects you with business professionals who can dispense advice and wisdom—and all at no charge. You get all that and more from SCORE, a nationwide association of retired and working volunteers, entrepreneurs, and corporate managers/executives.

Known as the "Counselors to America's Small Business," this resource partner of the SBA boasts 370 chapters nationwide that offer free one-on-one counseling to entrepreneurs, as well as online workshops on everything from entrepreneurship to small-business taxes, marketing, public relations, and more.

"After the workshops, you can grab a counselor and ask specific questions," says Merrily Schiavone, a Newark, Delaware consultant. "SCORE is just wonderful."

The organization's website (score.org) also is a treasure trove of information.

In addition to offering free e-newsletters, the site has loads of business resources, including business document templates, a financial management workbook, online workshops, and much more. You need to bookmark this valuable website. To contact SCORE, call (800) 634-0245 or e-mail at contactus@score.org.

Getting the
Word Out

Now that you have the basic structure of your new business established (or at least under construction), it's time to start marketing your services and capabilities to potential clients. After all, if your consulting business has no clients, then you have no business. But you must remember that selling your consulting services isn't the same as selling a car or a house. In the case of the car or the house, the customer is probably already in the market for one or both of those products. Your job is harder because you're marketing your services to people who may not even be aware they need those services.

There are a variety of methods with which you need to become both familiar and comfortable so you can get the word out about your business. Let's look at some of the conventional methods favored by consultants.

Direct Mail

Direct mail is a powerful way to drum up new business because it's targeted to exactly the audience you want to reach. You create or rent a targeted prospect list, send your prospective clients a sales letter, brochure, flier, or "lumpy envelope" (we'll discuss those later) describing the consulting services you offer, then sit back and wait for the calls to come in. OK, maybe it's not quite as simple as that. You also must do something to catch the attention of your prospects and pique their interest enough to make them want to call you. Otherwise, your direct mail piece will be just one more piece of junk mail that will end up under the Kit Kat candy wrappers in the "circular file."

Here are some tips for creating attention-getting direct mail:

- *Personalize your sales message.* Don't just send a brochure in a plain envelope and hope that the reader will be motivated to open it. Use a mail merge program and address each envelope to the recipient by name. In the same way, your sales letter inside the envelope should be directed to that recipient by name. "Dear Reader" mail is absolutely not acceptable if you want to pique the interest of potential clients.

- *Put a compelling message on the outside of the envelope.* "Free," "Limited time offer," and "Act now" are all powerful attention-getters that can induce the recipient to open the envelope. In addition, try mailing your message in something other than a standard #10 white envelope, because that will make the message stand out from the other mailing pieces in your prospect's mailbox.

- *Mail a "lumpy envelope."* This is a trick savvy marketers use that practically guarantees that their mail will be opened. The lumpiness comes from a free gift that has been enclosed in the envelope, which can be anything from a pen to a "gift card" good for a few hours of your time so the client can try you out. If at all possible, send a product that relates to your business, like, say, a personalized flash drive if you're a computer consultant. To find a product that would work for your particular consulting specialty, Google "advertising specialties" or "promotional advertising products."

- *Stress the benefits of your offer, and give all the pertinent details about it in your sales letter.* Then make it easy to respond or request information. Give your phone number, fax number, e-mail address, and website URL—and include a postage-paid postcard or envelope, too, so it's impossible *not* to get back to you if the interest is there.

- *Design a snappy, attention-getting piece.* Unless you have a marketing or advertising background, you may need help from a professional direct mail writer and/or graphic designer to come up with a sales letter or brochure that will dazzle your readers. Even though it's hard to part with the cash when you're launching your business, it's worth the money to get an experienced writer/designer team to create a provocative mailing piece. Think you'd like to tackle the job yourself? Then see page 89 for a sample brochure and page 87 for a sample direct mail letter.

- *Don't be discouraged if you get only a few responses.* Believe it or not, a 1 percent response to a direct mail piece is enough to make marketing pros do a little Snoopy dance of joy. Obviously, the more people you mail to, the better that 1 percent will look.

- *Mail regularly and often.* It takes time to establish your consulting "brand," so be sure to keep your message out there in front of your prospects. In addition, not everyone will be in the market for your services at the moment you contact them, so it's up to you to keep reminding them that you're ready and willing to work for them when they *are* ready.

> **Tip...**
>
> **Smart Tip**
> Affix postage stamps to direct mail envelopes rather than running the envelopes through a postage meter. This makes them look less like junk mail and more like something the recipient actually would want to open.

Identifying Your Target Market

So now you have a great mailing piece and high hopes for landing a lot of lucrative business. Your next step is to identify the right people to whom you should send your marketing pitches.

Back in Chapter 2, we discussed how to identify a market for your consulting services. This market should be broad enough to yield plenty of prospects, yet narrow enough to make sure you reach people who really will have a need for your services. Take some time to brainstorm and draw up a list of potential clients. Then start building your mailing list.

The obvious place to start is by compiling a list of names and addresses of every business contact and/or acquaintance you've encountered in your professional travels. But in the early days of your new venture, you may find that your network of prospects is rather limited. So you should consider buying a ready-made list of prospects to whom you can send mail or e-mail.

One of the easiest ways to find an appropriate mailing list is to go through a list broker. One that we know of offers access to 210 million consumers (which is more than two-thirds of the U.S. population). Its list is searchable by important demographics like geography, age, and income, and you have unlimited use of the list for a one-year period. To get the ball rolling, you tell the broker how many records you want to purchase, plunk down the cash, and mail away.

Because mailing lists are big business, there are many list brokers to choose from. But while you easily can find brokers by searching the internet, you might want to consult a publication like *Target Marketing* magazine for leads, since that's where the major (read: reputable) list brokers usually advertise. You can get a free subscription at targetmarketingmag.com. Alternately, you can check out the *Standard Rate and Data Service Directory* (SRDS), which is published by SRDS Media Solutions. This directory is a formidable database of up-to-date list rental information that's used by everyone from list brokers to mailers. But you don't have to pay the $715 single-use access fee—it's likely that a library in your local metropolitan area will have a current copy that you can peruse for free.

When considering who should populate your target market, unleash your creativity. Let's say your specialty is human resource consulting for small businesses. Clearly, the obvious market for your services would be small-business owners who may not be able to afford their own human resources department. But wait—there are many others who could benefit from your expertise, too. For instance, maybe Local Big Industry (automotive, high-tech, pharmaceutical, and others) is undergoing a transformation due to a slowing or booming economy. So pitch your services to any of the companies impacted by the economic climate, since they may find themselves in a position of having too much work to handle—or they may simply be in need of fresh, outside advice to help them weather the economic storm. Turn every opportunity into a lead and see where they take you.

> **Beware!**
> Mailing to the wrong list is the worst mistake a direct mailer can make when prospecting for business. Therefore, make sure you do the appropriate due diligence to identify the right prospect list so you don't waste money, time, and effort mailing to people who have no interest in your services.

> **Beware!**
> When you're building an e-mail contact list, include only those people who've given you permission to contact them. In this age of identity theft and Do Not Call lists, people are wary of unsolicited e-mail. Respect prospects' privacy, and you won't antagonize them unintentionally and damage your chances of building a future relationship.

Sample Direct Mail Letter

September 12, 2010

Dear Executive Director,

Did you know that in the next 90 days more than $10 million will be donated to nonprofit agencies in Delaware by local foundations? Do you know how to apply for your fair share of these funds?

My name is John Riddle, and I have more than 15 years' experience as a fundraising professional. I have worked at nonprofit agencies in Delaware, Maryland, and Pennsylvania as a development director, director of special events, and vice president of public relations.

If you need temporary fundraising help for a day, a week, or a few months, call me. As an experienced fundraising professional I can help you meet your fundraising goals by helping you with a plan of action that will work for your agency.

Sincerely,

John Riddle

John Riddle
Fundraising Consultant

Cold Calls

Another way to reach out to prospective clients is through cold calling, which is the process of contacting prospects who weren't expecting a sales call from you and trying to sell them on your services. Most people absolutely abhor cold calling, and in fact would rather give an oral presentation—naked—or have oral surgery than pitch their business by phone. But when you're starting a new consulting business, it's a good idea to try a mix of techniques to land new business, which means you should crank up your Bluetooth or put on your headset and give it a shot.

There are some ground rules for successful cold calling. First, be prepared to be rejected. It's nothing personal; it's just the way things work. Here's an example. Say you decide on a Monday morning to begin your day by making cold calls to obtain

▲

Brochure Basics

Your brochure should include these five elements.

1. Convey clearly what your services are.
2. Tell customers why you're the best.
3. Give a few reasons why you should be hired.
4. Include some brief biographical information.
5. Include some information about who your other clients are.

That's it. Keep it simple, but do it right. Remember, your brochure represents you in the marketplace, so make sure you polish it before you send it into action. Your entire consulting career depends on it.

the clients you need to keep your business in a healthy cash flow situation. To get at least one prospect to say yes, you may have to make between 20 and 30 contacts with people who have the authority to hire you.

Bright Idea

Ask your friends, neighbors, and business associates to save any direct mail pieces they have found interesting and were compelled to open. Start a file and save them, then review the file at least twice a year to generate new ideas that might work for you.

Yes, you read that correctly. To get at least one yes, you'll have to endure an awful lot of nos. Depending on your fee schedule, that figure could be even higher. To increase the chances of getting more yes responses, you must be flexible with your rates. In other words, do whatever it takes to grab that client, even if it means taking less money for the job. After all, that work could lead to repeat business or word-of-mouth referrals, which make that initial reduction in fees a lot easier to accept.

By the way, if you really hate making cold calls, you should know you're not alone. Merrily Schiavone, a Newark, Delaware consultant, is an experienced cold caller who once sold advertising. Yet she, too, dislikes picking up the phone and prospecting for work from people she doesn't know.

"I prefer to be in a situation where someone knows who I am, which is why I like networking instead," she says. "With networking, the people you meet typically are ready to request your services, and I get a lot of business that way. But cold calling is a necessary part of doing business that everyone needs to do."

Next, there are some things you can do to make the cold calling process easier. To begin with, try phoning business contacts between the hours of 6 and 8:30 a.m. A

Sample Brochure

Inside Flap   **Back Cover**   **Front Cover**

L R S MARKETING

GOES TO WORK AS YOUR:

- Project Planner
- Document Designer
- Writer
- Artist
- Publicity Partner
- Quality Assurance Team

We will be there for you!

L R S MARKETING INC.

L R S MARKETING INC.

MARKETING/
ADVERTISING
CONSULTANTS

"Reach For The Stars"

Tel: 302-994-2147

Inside Spread

ABOUT US...

L R S Marketing Inc. was founded in 1996. Its staff has over 23 years of marketing and advertising experience.

Since its founding in 1996, L R S Marketing has been devoted to upgrading the quality of marketing and advertising in this highly competitive market.

When you hire L R S Marketing, you're hiring a ready-made team of specialists that can make a difference in your business. All the components are in place: project manager, copy writers, editor, media and advertising consultants.

We hire experience, and all of us are great fun to work with.

Let L R S Marketing assist you in all the phases of marketing your company or products.

"Gentlemen start your engine"

WHAT WE DO...

We will meet with you to assure your comfort and satisfaction. Together with you, we create marketing and advertising that is unique, personal and profitable. We become involved in every aspect of the planning to provide you with the personal attention you deserve. L R S Marketing provides an invaluable service to companies. As full-time consultants, we concentrate on your needs. We have creativity, organizational skills and a very professional approach. These qualities are necessary to create the perfect plan!

"Golf with the Masters"

Project Planning And Management

We plan your documents, analyze the audience needs, define its contents, generate outlines, design the document, as well as schedule and budget the project.

Writing

L R S Marketing writes the drafts, revises text, incorporates review comments, writes the final draft and sends it off to the printer.

Editing

We edit the text for consistency, accuracy and usability. L R S will assist with preparing your artwork and integrating it with your text.

"And they're off"

Quality Assurance

We test your documents for accuracy and completeness.

L R S MARKETING INC.

1915 East Zabenko Drive
Wilmington, DE 19808
Phone: 302-994-2147
Fax: 302-994-2147
Email: Roxyl102@aol.com

lot of people arrive at the office early to catch up on work before the pressures of a normal day start mounting, so it can be a great time to catch someone when he or she might be more receptive to your sales pitch. Second, practice your pitch, both out loud and in front of a supportive business colleague or friend. Ask for feedback on the effectiveness and sincerity of your delivery, and make adjustments as necessary. Finally, set goals for yourself—say, two cold calls made twice a week. We guarantee that the more you call, the easier it will become—and you might even land some new business along the way.

> **! Beware!**
> If you're planning to use cold calling to solicit consumers for consulting services, you must register on the National Do Not Call Registry at https://telemarketing.donotcall.gov. Fees start at $55 per area code to check your call list against the Do Not Call registry. If you'll be making business-to-business calls, you can phone away without guilt (or fees).

John Riddle, the Bear, Delaware consultant, has pretty much mastered the art of cold calling, but he, too, has had to eat some costs to make a sale. When he was working as a fundraising consultant, for instance, he published a series of fundraising newsletters for the nonprofit industry. Every month, the newsletters had just one page of advertising for fundraising products and services of interest to people and organizations intent on raising money for various causes.

Riddle's usual way of soliciting advertising clients was via direct mail, and most months, he had no trouble selling enough ads to fill the page. But occasionally, he had to hustle and sell those ads by making cold calls.

The most effective pitch he ever made entailed telling potential customers there was only one quarter-page ad left and that the usual selling price for an ad of that size was $400. Then he would floor customers by saying they could name their own price for the space. Some people would pass on that incredible offer, but most could not resist, and the average offer he received for the space was $250 to $350. One potential advertiser offered a mere $25 for the ad space, but when Riddle asked him if that's all he thought his product was worth, the client ended up making a better offer.

> **! Beware!**
> Be sensitive to what time of day you make cold calls. Never call at dinnertime, and be aware of any difference in time zones. If you're not sure which time zone you're calling, plug the area code into an internet browser like Google, and voilà, you'll know whether you're calling Michigan or Montana.

The Dark Side of Cold Calling

Still not convinced that cold calling has value? Frank J. Rumbauskas Jr., author of the *New York Times* bestseller *Never Cold Call Again: Achieve Sales Greatness Without Cold Calling* (Wiley), agrees with you wholeheartedly. He believes that rather than making those dozens of contacts to get a single appointment with a qualified prospect, you can find better ways to spend your time that reap more rewards and are more appropriate for the twenty-first century. If you'd like to know more about Rumbauskas' take on cold calling, you can get a free preview edition (the first 10 chapters) of his book by signing up at nevercoldcall.com.

Dollar Stretcher

Contact publications directed at your target audience to see if they have any special advertising sections scheduled for production in the next few months. They almost always do, and they may have special discount advertising rates. Trade newspapers and journals are the best places to start your search.

Warming Up to Cold Calls

There are a couple tricks you can use to make cold calling a little easier:

- *Prepare a script ahead of time.* Write out word-for-word what you expect to say when you get someone on the telephone. Remember, though, that your goal is to get a face-to-face interview and, eventually, a new client. So before you end up stumbling over your sales presentation (either in person or over the telephone), practice it again and again.

- *Be creative in your efforts to reach the decision-maker.* Most times you'll encounter a secretary or administrative assistant who has years of experience turning away cold callers like yourself. But don't give up. (One of Winston Churchill's favorite sayings was "Never give up, never give up, never ever give up!" It's good advice.) To avoid being screened by the secretary, try calling before or after business hours. You may have to call before 8 a.m. or after 5 p.m., but at these times, chances are the decision-makers you're trying to reach will answer their own phones.

▲

Advertising

Because traditional advertising can be expensive, it's important to spend your advertising dollars wisely. Jeff Bartlett, a Harrisburg, Pennsylvania marketing research consultant, maximizes his advertising dollars by advertising only in the publication produced by an association to which he belongs. "The association publishes what is called the *Green Book*, which is a directory of research and marketing consulting businesses around the country," he says. "It has helped me generate new business."

Other consultants, such as Schiavone, depend on word-of-mouth. "The best form of advertising [for my business] has been word-of-mouth and recommendations from other people," she says. "I've found that being active in organizations like the chamber of commerce generates a lot of leads."

You may find that all you have to do to get your business rolling is to advertise early in your new career. "When I started out, I wanted to work in the nonprofit field so I initially did some advertising," says Bill Metten, a Hockessin, Delaware public relations consultant. "But I wasn't after high-profile clients, and the state is so small that everyone knows everyone else. So now I rely on word-of-mouth to land new business."

Depending on the type of services you offer, it may be necessary to advertise in specialized trade journals or magazines. Before you spend any money on this, start looking through back issues of professional journals and newspapers related to the fields you specialize in. If you don't subscribe to those journals or newspapers, visit your nearest university or college library, since chances are good they'll have them in their collection. Note how many times other consultants have placed those ads. What type of ads did they use? Did they place large display ads? Or did they limit themselves to smaller ads in the publications' classified sections? Do they use clip art, or are the ads all type? How effective are the ads, in your opinion?

After examining these materials, you can start making decisions about your own advertising efforts. Feel free to adapt the best ideas for use in your ads. Just be careful not to plagiarize anyone else's work.

In addition to placing ads in the full print run of a publication, you also should consider advertising in any specialty sections that might include a "Consultants Directory" or "Directory of Consulting Services." (Consulting professionals like Riddle stress that directory advertising is well worth the cost.) To find out if your target publication plans to produce a directory of consulting services, contact its advertising department, and ask for an editorial calendar. Keep in mind, though, that publications can have lead times of as much as six months, so be sure to call for a copy of the editorial calendar no later than August or September if you think you'd like to advertise during the following year.

Another useful though expensive advertising tool is your local Yellow Pages. You'll automatically receive a line ad (consisting of your company name and phone number) in the Yellow Pages when you install a business phone line, but you might want to consider taking a larger ad in the book.

To determine whether you should advertise, take a look at your local telephone book to see what types of consultants have already placed ads there. Also, when you're at the library looking through back issues of those professional publications mentioned earlier, browse through some telephone books from other cities (you can usually find a large collection of telephone books in the reference section). Again, take a look at the ads and listings in the Yellow Pages that feature consultants and consulting services. When you first opened a page that listed consultants, did your eyes go directly to the display ads, which are the largest ads on the page? Probably. That's what a display ad is supposed to do—catch your eye and say "Hey, read me first!" The psychology is simple. By virtue of its size alone, a larger ad will attract more potential clients than a regular classified listing ever will.

There's another benefit to taking a display ad: People may assume that since you've spent extra money on that display ad, you may be more established and even more professional than those consultants who didn't opt for the large ad. So although you'll probably want to start with a smaller, more affordable display ad, if your budget permits, you might want to experiment with different sizes of display ads and see which one draws in the most business.

There's one caveat when it comes to Yellow Pages advertising. There are so many phone companies these days, each with their own directories, that it can be difficult to know which one to choose. "I think the usefulness of a Yellow Pages ad is directly related to geography," says Huntington Beach, California consultant Susan Bock. "In a smaller area, it might be useful. But if your area has different service providers and each city has its own phone book, it can be hard to justify the cost of advertising in all of them."

Newsletters

Newsletters can be an effective tool when it comes to rounding up clients for your consulting business. Through newsletters, you can present news of interest to potential clients and remind former clients that you're still alive and kicking—and available if they need help again.

When Riddle started as a fundraising consultant, he decided that publishing a variety of fundraising newsletters was the most effective way to sign up new clients. So he began mailing a free six-month subscription to local nonprofit agencies he thought might benefit the most from his newsletter and might be good candidates to use his consulting services. Because he controlled the articles that appeared in each issue, he could use the space to tell of successes he'd achieved as a fundraising consultant for other nonprofits.

Anatomy of a Newsletter

A typical newsletter published by a consultant will include:

- *News of importance to the industry:* You can collect information from a variety of sources, including magazines, newspapers, professional journals, websites, etc. Just make sure you credit the source of each news item you use.
- *Editorials and opinions:* Here's your chance to sound off on a particular subject related to your consulting field.
- *Tips for success:* Tell your readers how they can do their jobs better.

His strategy paid off. Within the first year, Riddle received consulting contracts from four nonprofit organizations—all because they had been on his free mailing list. This is a strategy you can use, too!

Newsletters are usually four pages long, which gives you plenty of room to experiment with different types of articles that subtly sell your services while providing information the reader can use. If you work in a technical field like computer consulting, a newsletter can be a smart way to showcase your knowledge—and generate new business. For instance, David McMullen, a Costa Mesa, California computer consultant, e-mails a two-page newsletter to a list of about 350 clients and prospects. It's full of tips for fixing problems or working more efficiently, plus it serves as a reminder to anyone who hasn't used his services for a while to call if they have a technology problem.

Whatever your consulting field is, you should have more than enough information to produce a newsletter that can be used to attract potential clients. If you don't have the time or don't feel comfortable self-publishing your newsletter, hire a local freelance writer and graphic designer to do the job for you. Your newsletter doesn't have to be an expensive, four-color, glossy publication. In fact, the simpler it is, the better. A good newsletter will sell itself based on the content rather than on a splashy design.

To get some ideas, start collecting newsletters published in your field. If you're not familiar with any, go to EzineLocater at ezinelocater.com, or Newsletter Access at newsletteraccess.com, both of which are searchable databases of newsletters that also

Bright Idea

If you're planning to send out your newsletter electronically, keep it to two pages. Surveys show that people really hate scrolling when reading on a computer screen, so don't inundate them with a lot of pages. Instead, e-mail news more often if you have more to discuss than can be covered in those two pages.

include contact information. Then write or e-mail the publishers of newsletters you're interested in and ask for sample copies before you design and write your first issue.

Don't underestimate the power of a newsletter. The last time you received one in the mail, did you put it aside to read later? And why did you do that? Probably because you wanted to make sure you weren't missing any important news or information. And what about that brochure you received in the mail the same day? Did you put it aside to read later or did it go directly into the trash can? Think about that before you spend big bucks on a glitzy brochure.

Referrals

This often-overlooked method of finding new clients is such an easy marketing activity that you may be stunned that you didn't think of it yourself. All you have to do is wait until you've finished your consulting assignment, confirm that your client is completely satisfied, then ask for a referral. Rather than putting your client on the spot, just send a note or a short letter to him or her asking for the names of any colleagues, friends, or business associates who might be good prospects for your consulting services.

Chances are good you'll get some excellent leads, as David McMullen has discovered. He even goes so far as to tell each client that referrals are his only source of new business and that he would be very appreciative if they passed his name on to someone who could use his services. "If everyone I know sent me one name," he says, "I'd have more work than I'd know what to do with."

It's also a nice idea to send a letter to clients on their birthdays—or to mark another momentous occasion—to wish

▲

them a happy day and remind them that (1) ou appreciate their business and (2) you're available for additional work. The sample special occasion letter below is one you can adapt for your own use.

A simple thank-you letter sent to express your appreciation for a client's business is also a good way to stay on his or her radar, especially since few businesspeople take the time to follow up this way. You'll find a sample letter you can use on the next page.

Sample Special Occasion Letter

LRS Marketing, Inc.

1000 East Culver Dr.
Wilmington, CA 90006
(949) 857-2000
LRSmarketing@aol.com

February 11, 2010

Robin Passwater
Alarm Data Corp.
2500 Eastburn Dr.
Irvine, CA 91000

Dear Robin,

Happy birthday!

Please accept our wishes for an enjoyable day and a prosperous year.

We also want to take this opportunity to thank you for your business. Customers like you make it all worthwhile.

With warm regards,

R.S. Walker

R.S. Walker
President
LRS Marketing Inc.

LRS Marketing, Inc.

1000 East Culver Dr.
Wilmington, CA 90006
(949) 857-2000
LRSmarketing@aol.com

February 11, 2010

Randy Reed
ADT Security Service Inc.
18 Boulder St.
Tustin, CA 91720

Dear Randy,

Thank you for participating in the Home Show at the Concord Mall on May 20–23 and for choosing to do business with LRS Marketing Inc.

Our goal is to serve clients to the best of our ability. If we find more opportunities for your company to exhibit its product, we will notify you.

It was a privilege to work with you!

Sincerely,

R.S. Walker

R.S. Walker
President
LRS Marketing Inc.

Meeting Your
Public

As you already know from Chapter 9, there are a lot of things you can do to advertise your business, from sending out direct mail pieces to cold calling. But there's another way to spread the news about your services and capabilities that often costs little or nothing, yet can yield big benefits. What we're talking about is public relations, which is self-promotion that tells prospective clients who you are, how wonderful you are, and what you can do for them.

To the modest among us, that might sound like shameless spin-doctoring. But the truth is, PR is an effective way to create a strong, positive, and controlled message about your business. Marketing gurus say that when messages like these are conveyed in news articles, they come across as more credible to the public than messages in paid-for ads. So feel free to use the various PR tools available to you to generate positive press—it's standard operating procedure for businesses and when done well, a new client magnet.

One of the things that sets PR apart from advertising is that it's not a sure thing. With advertising, you pay for the ad or direct mail piece or radio commercial, and it runs in the medium of your choice. With PR, you create the buzz and excitement about some positive aspect of your business through a carefully crafted printed piece or through word-of-mouth, then wait and hope that some savvy newspaper or magazine editor will be intrigued enough to publish something about it. The trick is to make the information so interesting and compelling that those media types eventually will look forward to what you're going to say next—or may even call or e-mail you for more information. Here's an example: When CNN or Money.com needs a sound bite or insight on financial matters, their producers often call on Douglas Flynn, a certified financial planner with Flynn Zito Capital Management LLC in New York. Flynn consults on a wide range of financial matters, so he's been interviewed by or featured in various publications, from the *Wall Street Journal* and *New York Times Magazine* to *Self, Parents Magazine*, and many others.

The point is, you want to be "in like Flynn," so to speak; i.e., the person the local media turns to for commentary about your area of expertise. Public relations strategies like the ones discussed in this chapter can help you get there.

News Releases

One of the simplest and most cost-effective forms of publicity at your disposal is the news release. Also known as press releases, these one- to two-page documents are sent out by companies and business professionals to tell the world about their new products and services, as well as to remind them how good they are at what they do. In a way, they're little advertisements for your business, except they don't cost you a thing beyond the time it takes to write them and the necessary production expenses such as stationery, envelopes, and postage. And since editors generally prefer to receive releases by e-mail these days, they're about as close to free as you can get.

Generally speaking, newspaper and magazine editors use news releases as filler material. They also use them as idea starters that can be developed into related or more detailed stories. Because news releases are used on a space-available basis, there's no guarantee that yours will get into print. But that doesn't mean you shouldn't keep trying, because when one does hit print, the evening TV news, or drive-time radio, it's free publicity.

Even if you're not a writer by trade, you can put together a simple news release. To start the process, think like a reporter and consider the six questions a journalist asks: who, what, where, when, why, and how. Jot down your thoughts related to each of those questions, then choose the most important thing you want the reader to know. That becomes the lead for the release, and it's important to put this main point up front since editors tend to cut copy from the end of a release if it's too long to run in its entirety. Then fill in with other important details, and you're good to go.

News releases have a standard format that should be used so anyone who opens the envelope or reads the e-mail will know what he or she is looking at. They also should be only about a page long since brevity appeals to busy editors and journalists.

By the way, it used to be common practice after sending a news release to make a courtesy call to the editor(s) to whom you sent the release to ask whether it was received. But let's face it: Unless the U.S. Post Office decided to stop delivering mail in your state or your ISP unexpectedly exploded, then of course it was received. And if you want to know the truth, editors hate it when you call and ask that question. The real question is, "Can you use this information?" The best way to find that out is to call first to pitch your idea, then follow up with a news release that has all the details.

Now, we know what you're thinking: "Oh, no, more cold calling!" And yes, you're right about that. But as mentioned in Chapter 9, cold calling is a necessary evil for drumming up new business, and the same thing goes for pitching your story ideas. Pitching in advance of writing also means you won't waste your time crafting the perfect news release, then never seeing a single one hit print.

> **Tip...**
>
> **Smart Tip**
> It's appropriate these days to pitch your idea on an editor's or reporter's voice mail. Just be sure to give sufficient information (but keep your message to about two to three points) and provide full contact information so the person can get back to you if the idea has merit or fits the editorial mix.

> **Tip...**
>
> **Smart Tip**
> Some of the things you can write releases about include anything newsworthy, especially things that will help the reader do something better-smarter-faster-cheaper, and any interesting or unusual accomplishments or services you offer. The operative word here is "newsworthy." If the news isn't interesting to anyone except you, then it shouldn't go out in a news release.

Media Lists

Of course, those news releases need to be e-mailed or snail mailed to someone, so you'll need to develop your own customized media list. To build your list, start by checking websites or calling for the editorial calendars and contact lists for your local media. That way, when you're ready to send something to the press, you have the name of the reporter or editor you need to contact. (Before you actually send out your release, make a quick telephone call to the source to verify the contact name. It's not unusual to find that an editor has either moved on to a new assignment or has left that organization altogether.)

The easiest way to build a media list is to use a website like mondotimes.com, which lists all the print, TV, and radio outlets worldwide. (For instance, a search for "New Mexico major new media" turned up the *Albuquerque Journal*, the *Las Cruces Sun-News*, and the *Santa Fe New Mexican*.) You'll also find clickable links that will take you to the publication's or broadcast station's website, where you can find the contact info you need. You may have to call to obtain the name of the editor or assignment editor who would be the recipient of your releases. Additional sources for media lists are your local chamber of commerce, the department of tourism (also known as the convention and visitors bureau in some states), or FinderBinder (finderbinder.com), which publishes media directories for some of the largest media markets in the United States.

Keep in mind, there are some important publications that don't appear on standard media lists: namely, corporate and business newsletters. Virtually all large companies publish some type of internal employee newsletter or bulletin, which can be great to include in your PR campaign. In addition to featuring news and information of interest to their employees, most of these publications include community news and a calendar of events. So if you're interested in plumbing this market, check with the human resources departments of the companies you're targeting to see if they have such publications.

Here's a story about how company publications helped John Riddle when he worked as a fundraising consultant in Bear, Delaware. A client hired him to produce a special event he had dreamed up: an attempt to make the *Guinness Book of World Records* by having the largest group of people ever dance the Twist at one time. The idea was to charge people $5 each and have them come to a local racetrack and enjoy music, food, and fun in a picnic grove.

> **Tip...**
>
> **Smart Tip**
> Check with your local media contacts to see if they prefer to have news releases and public service announcements sent via e-mail, fax, or snail mail. By working with the media on their terms, you're enhancing your chances of getting the coverage you desire.

Bright Idea

You can save money on the cost of producing a client newsletter by having a professional designer create a simple two-page newsletter template, then simply plugging in the text and/or photographs yourself when you're ready to publish a new edition.

While local newspapers and radio stations gave the event some coverage a few days before the event, Riddle had enormous success from the press releases and stories he submitted to various corporate newsletters in town. Before long, advance ticket sales were going strong, and his client began getting calls from those corporate employees who wanted to volunteer for their organization not only at that event but at future ones, as well. The corporations also bought large blocks of tickets (at $5 each) to distribute to their employees. As a result, the event was a huge hit all around.

Check out the "Talking Points" chapter in *Startup Basics* for more publicity tips.

Public Speaking

Public speaking is another excellent way to recruit new clients and to earn a reputation for excellence in your community. Unless you live in a town so small it doesn't have a chamber of commerce or a Lions Club, Rotary Club, or similar service organiza-

Beware!

If you make a mistake that results in a missed deadline or poor performance on the job, don't try to sidestep blame. Admit your responsibility, apologize, and ask how you can rectify the situation. Then do whatever it takes to make the client happy, even if it means putting in extra time on the job without payment. It's the best way to negate bad publicity.

tion, you can begin offering your services as a speaker for luncheons, dinners, or other special occasions.

Susan Bock, a Huntington Beach, California, human resources consultant, does this successfully. She does a lot of public speaking for professional organizations on topics ranging from empowerment and team building to organizational effectiveness, interviewing techniques, and diversity training. In addition to delivering her wisdom to groups as small as a dozen people and as large as several hundred, Bock also uses the occasions to prospect for new clients.

"I leave materials on each of the tables that include a biography tailored to the audience and an invitation for a free consultation," she says. "Take-away materials like these are crucial because many of these talks are scheduled during evening meetings when people are tired after a long day at the office. If they have something to take away with them, they're more likely to call at a future time."

Riddle also has used his experience as a public speaker to land new clients. As a fundraising consultant, he often was asked to speak to organizations about the successful projects for which he has raised money. On several occasions, there were people in the audience who were volunteers or board members from other nonprofit organizations, and when the function was over, they approached him about working as a consultant for their agency. So unless you're deathly afraid of public speaking (and you'd better not be, because as a consultant, you will be presenting oral and written reports to your clients), get busy and start contacting those local service organizations. To find them, use the telephone directory, go to WhitePages.com, or ask around to find out if anyone has published a directory of service organizations in your community. You also can visit the library and ask at the reference desk. Make a list of organizations that hold monthly meetings and therefore may use guest speakers. Contact each group and offer your services.

Teaching a Workshop

One surefire way to discover if the field you've chosen is one in which you'll succeed is to put together enough material to teach a workshop. It doesn't have to be anything fancy—just a talk that will hold people's attention and give them some good information in your area of expertise.

It's possible to turn any topic, interest, or specialty into a workshop, as Riddle discovered. He had struggled for nearly five years to become a freelance writer without successfully publishing anything. Then one day he read an article in *Writer's Digest* about how newspapers and magazines were always on the lookout for freelance writers to write book reviews. The advice worked. A few weeks after he read that article (which he now uses as a handout in his writing workshops), his first book review was published, and it opened up many other publishing opportunities. So Riddle decided to offer a workshop for beginning freelance writers, which he called "Introduction to Freelance Writing." The local school district was delighted to include the workshop in its adult education catalog, and Riddle found himself teaching for the first time in his life.

Tip...

Smart Tip
Service organizations that are always looking for public speakers include:

- American Legion
- Lions Club
- Rotary Club
- Kiwanis Club
- Elks Lodge
- Chambers of commerce
- Masons
- YMCA/YWCA
- PTA/PTO organizations
- VFW chapters

If you're passionate and knowledgeable about your chosen consulting field, you, too, should be able and willing to present a workshop on it. After all, you just might meet people in your workshop who one day could use your consulting services or will refer you to someone else who can. Plus, the added visibility is always a good thing for your business, so try developing a workshop—it could be your ticket to increased profits.

Hitting the Lecture Circuit

Making contact with organizations and associations that would be interested in having you address their monthly membership meetings or other special events is just the first step in landing speaking engagements that can increase your visibility. It's also a good idea to come up in advance with several viable lecture topics to pitch to those groups, as well as handouts or other materials you might like to distribute. That way, you'll be ready on a moment's notice to fill a vacant slot on a meeting agenda.

Because there are bound to be people in the audience who either could use someone with your particular expertise or who know someone else who's looking for a consultant, be sure to tell the audience during your presentation that you're a consultant in the (fill-in-the-blank) field, then use examples and stories in your talk directly related to your field. Also, always take a generous supply of your business cards and brochures along with you and leave them on the table next to the podium where you're speaking. Anyone who comes up to speak to you afterward will certainly pick them up.

Networking

If you expect to do business in your community, consider joining one or more professional business organizations. These groups provide you with opportunities to meet other members (some of whom may need your services), serve on committees, and otherwise gain visibility and credibility among business acquaintances. Among the organizations that have excellent networking potential are the chamber of commerce, the Rotary Club, and any local economic development group.

"Networking is a real art, and many chambers of commerce hold seminars to teach you how to do it," says Newark, Delaware consultant Merrily Schiavone. "They teach you how to ask the right questions, how to pitch your own company in 30 seconds, and how to know when to move on if it doesn't look like your services will be needed. A new consultant will find this information very valuable."

Riddle has used his memberships in professional associations to great advantage. As a member of the National Society of Fundraising Executives and the Delaware Association of Nonprofit Agencies, he was able to keep in touch with the majority of the people and nonprofit agencies within the state of Delaware. By developing this network of contacts and attending various luncheons and other events, he has obtained plenty of contracts.

Melinda Patrician, a consultant in Arlington, Virginia, also believes that it's important to join associations in your field. "As a public relations consultant who has done work for many book publishers, I keep in touch with people in the industry," she says.

The point is, you can't just sit in your office, send out brochures, and expect people to beat down your door. You need to get out and be with people—especially those who could use your consulting services. "Successful consultants network like crazy," says Colorado market research consultant Carol Monaco. "Do some volunteer work, join business organizations, sit on their boards of directors, and get to know a lot of people, because that's the way to get business."

To find out which associations have a chapter in your city or town, check your local library for a copy of the *Encyclopedia of Associations: National Organizations of the United States* (Gale Research), which lists 22,500 nonprofit membership organizations. Browse through the listings, which are alphabetized by association as well as grouped by subject matter, and copy down names and telephone numbers of those you would like to contact. Then follow through and sign up with the organizations that interest you most. If you come across an association that doesn't have a group meeting where you live, you might consider starting a local chapter. What better way to attract potential clients?

Of course, the whole point of joining organizations is to network with other business professionals at group functions. When you arrive for a luncheon meeting or other event, circulate widely and pass out your business card every time you make a new acquaintance. But don't just blatantly come out and say you're looking for new business ("Hi, my name is Veronica Banish. I'm an image consultant and you look like you could really use help picking your wardrobe. Call me."). Rather, introduce yourself and mention what you do. Then stick to the kind of small talk you'd exchange at a cocktail party. If the conversation turns to business, so much the better. Then you can commiserate about small-business issues like tax rates or hiring difficulties or time management challenges. The idea is to lay the groundwork for future business relationships, since after you see the same

Tip...

Smart Tip

A great way to position yourself as a specialist in your field is to sign up with ProfNet, an online network of business professionals who wish to be contacted by journalists looking for expert commentary. For a fee, ProfNet will post your biography and forward media inquiries from reporters looking for sources. For more information, go to profnet.com.

Bright Idea

Check the calendar sections of your local newspapers and magazines, which usually list clubs and organizations that are having meetings and luncheons. A telephone number and a contact name will probably be listed, too, so take advantage of this free networking resource.

people a few times, they'll know who you are and probably will be inclined to call you when the need for your type of service arises.

Finally, keep an eye out for special networking meetings held by organizations like the chamber of commerce. The sole purpose of these types of meetings is to get people together to exchange information and business cards, so you don't have to be shy about self-promotion. Just keep in mind that everyone else there will be doing the same thing, which can be counterproductive if you're trying to network at a meeting comprised solely of, say, computer consultants or communication consultants. In essence, you'll be networking with your competitors, who are not very likely to use your services or refer you to someone else.

Dr. Linda Henman, a strategy coach in St. Louis and author of *The Magnetic Boss* (EFG Publishing), networks with her peers in a way. She belongs to what she calls a "mastermind group," consisting of three women who offer many of the same, though not competing, services. "We have monthly telephone conferences during which we each have 30 minutes to discuss whatever we want," she says. "Looking at a situation through their eyes has earned and saved me thousands of dollars. It's often the best 90 minutes of my month."

When Things Go Wrong

Most of the time, your contact with the media will be positive. But if you ever have a problem with a client (because of something the client or you did), you may find yourself dealing with the media in less than desirable circumstances. Since damage control is a part of the overall PR function, it's important to know what to do in the event of a business misstep or an outright PR disaster.

To begin with, keep in mind that it's best not to avoid the media or sidestep their questions. The more you avoid them, the worse it will be, and the fallout from even the smallest hint of scandal can spell disaster for your business. By all means, you want to avoid being the lead story on page one or on the six o'clock news because people tend to remember bad stories.

With that in mind, you should have a disaster plan ready to use in the event something goes wrong. Here are some guidelines you can use to deflect unexpected bad press:

- Always keep the media well informed of all developments in a story.

- Don't make the media wait for answers to their questions; they may find their own sources for answers, and those other sources may not be accurate.

- Use only facts. Don't give theories, conjectures, or anything else besides the facts.

- Update information as often as possible.

- Maintain a professional attitude.

- Have only one person in charge to answer questions from reporters.

Bright Idea

Colorado market research consultant Carol Monaco recommends making an effort to get to know your clients personally. "Develop a relationship with them, take them to lunch, ask them about their family," she says. "A consultant is a lone wolf—you need other people to keep you going. Plus people buy from people they like."

These are simple yet effective ways to build a public image that can make you look like an expert in your field. So before you plunk down all those advertising dollars to promote your business, try some of these techniques instead so you can save your startup bucks to set up a website (discussed in Chapter 11) and the other things you'll need to make your business run efficiently and profitably.

Casting Your (Inter)net

It wasn't so long ago that having a presence on the internet was a choice rather than a necessity for a new business. But that was then. Today, you're selling yourself short if you don't have a website, because people pretty much expect you to be out there when they're searching for information at all hours of the day or night. If your website does not pop up on a search engine, those prospective customers will search elsewhere—and you won't even know what a great opportunity you've missed to make some money or expand your business.

And of course, there are other interactive tools like Facebook and Twitter that started as social networking pages but are now important tools for business owners. So this chapter will look at the various ways you can launch your business into cyberspace and make sure your cyber presence is working hard for you at any given moment, even if in reality, you happen to be on the golf course, in a business meeting, or at your child's piano recital.

Test the Waters

Before you leap into the webpage design process and design a full-blown site with complex navigation, it's a good idea to see what your competition is doing so you know what you're up against. For example, you might find that your closest competitors have simple static websites, which are sites with noninteractive content. These types of sites, which are also known as business card or brochure sites, display the same information to every visitor. This information usually includes basics like a list of the services the business offers and how it can be contacted. Static websites may have features like Flash content (i.e., streaming or moving video and pictures) and photos, but essentially they're meant to be cyber bookmarks.

On the other hand, you might find that your competition has dynamic websites, which are sites that have an established design but can be updated, amended, or otherwise changed as necessary. This type of website is a better choice than a static website because if you plan to post articles (either those you write or those you post with permission), sell merchandise (say, copies of your bestselling consulting book), or host a blog, you'll need the extra capabilities of a dynamic website. Of course, there's more to managing this type of website than a static site, but you don't necessarily have to do the work yourself if you have a budget to hire a web consultant. Plus, if your competition has static sites, yours will really stand out if it changes by virtue of updated content.

Here's some of the content you can choose to include on your website:

- List of services
- Biography
- Resources
- FAQs
- Industry-specific articles
- Events (including your teaching or speaking schedule)
- Pressroom (copies of news releases or articles written about you)
- Store (sell your books and books related to your field, or other materials)
- Blog (let your public know what you're doing and thinking)
- Contact information

But that's just the tip of the consulting iceberg, so to speak. Consultants like Merrily Schiavone in Newark, Delaware use their websites as portfolios of their work. "I often direct prospects who contact me for information or a quote to my website so they can see what type of work I've done," Schiavone says. "In fact, sometimes when I'm on the phone with prospective clients, I tell them to log on so we can both look at the same sample while we're talking. Clients like having that option very much."

For more help deciding what should be included on your site, check out the website design questionnaire used by Elbel Consulting Services LLC that appears on pages 118–121. Owner Fred Elbel asks his new website design clients to fill out the form so he can design a site that meets their expectations perfectly.

One valuable thing a professional designer like Fred Elbel can do is to create a site that matches the sophistication of potential users. You'd think that practically everyone would have at least a working knowledge of the internet these days. But that isn't necessarily the case, as John Riddle in Bear, Delaware found out the hard way. When he decided to sell a fundraising plan he called the "No Go, No Show" campaign, he designed several greeting cards that nonprofit organizations all across the country could use to solicit contributions for their causes. The cards were meant to be used to invite potential donors to an imaginary New Year's Eve dinner party. But instead of attending yet another boring rubber chicken affair, the donor had the luxury of making a contribution and staying home instead. The key to the campaign's success was the way humor was used throughout the card and the reply card the donors used when they sent in their checks.

Riddle hired a website designer who took his rough drawings and instructions and turned them into an award-winning website. The pages were colorful, interesting, and filled with free fundraising advice people could use by just visiting the site. Each fundraising plan came complete with sample cards, instructions, and a toll-free number to call. Convinced he was the king of customer service, Riddle registered the website with the appropriate search engines and waited for the money to start rolling in. But although the site received several hundred hits per day from visitors all across the United States and even a half-dozen foreign countries, no one placed an order.

"I had forgotten the most important rule when it comes to marketing via the internet: Your target audience had to be both online and internet-savvy," Riddle

Smart Tip

A survey by Hitwise, an online intelligence service, indicated that nearly 71 percent of internet searches are performed through Google. But it can pay to register your website on as many search engines as possible. An easy and fast way to get the worldwide attention you crave is to use a service like Add Me (addme.com), which charges a small fee to register your site with numerous search engines worldwide.

says. "But in this case, my target audience for the 'No Go, No Show' fundraising plan was small and midsized social service nonprofit organizations, most of which barely had computers at the time, let alone internet access. Eventually, I realized this and pulled the website."

Since internet access and usage are now ubiquitous, this probably won't happen to you. Just consider the numbers. A recent Harris Interactive survey determined that in 2008, 81 percent of U.S. adults are now online, up from just 9 percent in 1995. That's 184 million adult Americans who are now online. Of these users, 31 percent are college graduates, and 64 percent have household incomes above $50,000. In addition, 65 percent of people aged 18 to 49 are online, which is significant because they're likely to be the main users of consulting services.

By Design

Here are some elements you might consider including on your web page:

- *Flash intro:* This is a great tool for consultants who sell a "sexy" product or service (computer consultants and image consultants come to mind). Flash is an attention-getting tool that consists of moving images and/or audio sound bites meant to catch surfers' attention. If you decide to use Flash, be sure to place a "skip intro" option on the Flash page so eager (or impatient) readers can bypass your artwork and get to the point. For an example of an elaborate Flash intro, check out the very cool—though not overdone—Flash intro on the website of RMH Telecom Consultants at rmhtc.com.

- *Service "menu":* This page should describe in detail every service you offer. This is useful for two reasons: It gives surfers enough information to know whether they should contact you directly, and it allows you to suggest other services the customer might be interested in. Incidentally, it's not necessary to give prices on this page. It's almost always better to request that they call you to discuss their project before you divulge any financial details.

- *Portfolio:* As Schiavone mentioned, an online portfolio allows you to show actual samples of the work you've done. It's particularly useful for people who provide visual and communications arts services, but it also can be used by consultants in other fields whose completed projects can be photographed and downloaded to the site.

Bright Idea

When writing copy for your website, keep it brief enough so each topic will fit on one screen, since many people find it annoying to have to keep scrolling down as they read.

- *Biography:* If you have impressive credentials from previous corporate work or other projects, you might want to write a paragraph or two about your experience, since it may convince prospects that their work will be in good hands.

- *List of clients:* You might consider adding this later after you've gotten some successful jobs under your belt. If you can drop the names of a couple big-name clients, so much the better. Just be sure to ask each client's permission to use his or her name before publishing the information for all to see.

- *Contact information:* In addition to providing a phone and a fax number, it's a good idea to include an e-mail address for those who prefer making a cyber contact. Thanks to e-mail, you can do business with anyone anywhere in the world, so it's not necessary to divulge your location or mailing address on this page.

No matter what you decide to put on your site, make sure you update the information regularly so clients keep coming back. "I redo my website completely about every two years to keep it fresh and current," says Huntington Beach, California consultant Susan Bock. "My site is designed for and targeted to prospective clients, and keeping it current lends credibility to what I do."

Building Your Site

While it can be tempting to put up one of the free basic websites available online or from your ISP just to have something online, for the most professional results you should leave the job of creating a website to an experienced web developer. In addition to understanding the basics of HTML, the language of websites, and all the technical aspects involved in building a site, a developer can advise you on technicalities like how information should be packaged for maximum impact and how to optimize text with keyword phrases to get a high search engine ranking. A developer also can set the site up so you can update it yourself or add new content easily.

Generally speaking, this is not a job for an amateur. "The truth is, most people don't have the technical skills or the time to produce a good website," says Fred Elbel, the Colorado computer consultant. "Your website is an extension of your marketing plan and has to be a notch above your competition, plus optimizing a website for success is an art and a science. Most people don't have the skill or time to do all that."

The cost of a professionally designed, fully functional website is based on factors like the number of pages on the site and the amount of artwork or photos used, and typically will range from $1,000 to $3,500. A template-based site with just a few pages usually will run under $1,000. It's customary for web designers to charge by the hour for future maintenance and/or updates on the site, which is a good reason to ask your designer to create a site that you can update yourself. To find a web designer, check the Yellow Pages, or contact your local chamber of commerce or other business organization.

Site Seeing

The internet is not only a great place to get your name in front of potential clients—it's chock full of resources to help you in your business as well. The array of information can be overwhelming, but here are a few websites to get you started:

- *AARP (aarp.org):* provides information and resources for people age 50+
- *Amazon (amazon.com):* huge online seller of books, CDs, DVDs, and more
- *CPA Finder (cpafinder.com):* a listing of accountants by state
- *eBay (ebay.com):* an amazing resource for buying or selling just about anything, from office equipment to office supplies
- *Entrepreneur (entrepreneur.com):* the premier source for small-business advice
- *FindLaw (findlaw.com):* a legal source with free information, tools, and resources, as well as an attorney finder
- *Health Insurance In-Depth (healthinsuranceindepth.com):* a source for information about insurance basics and free health insurance comparison quotes
- *IRS (irs.ustreas.gov):* the official source for tax tips, advice, and publications; also helpful is irs.gov/smallbiz, which has a wealth of info for small business owners
- *National Association for the Self-Employed (nase.org):* offers advice, access to health insurance, and more
- *National Association of Women Business Owners (nawbo.org):* acts as the voice of more than 10 million women-owned businesses and offers business resources and tools
- *National Small Business Network (businessknowhow.net):* a great source for free business information
- *SBA (sbaonline.sba.gov):* an invaluable resource for everything related to starting a small business
- *U.S. Census Bureau (census.gov):* the government site for demographic and other population information
- *USPS ZIP code lookup (zip4.usps.com/zip4/welcome.jsp):* a useful resource for direct-mail efforts
- *Verizon's area code lookup (www22.verizon.com/areacodes/):* allows you to look up area codes by state or figure out where you're calling by area code

Despite having said all that about using a computer pro, we do understand that you may not have the cash to hire a consultant right away. So if you have the time and patience to take on the job yourself, you could try creating your own simple website. There are a number of web design programs on the market, like Adobe Dreamweaver (retails for $399) which can make the job easy for anyone who's at least somewhat computer savvy.

Once your website is operational, you'll have to select an internet host site, which is the place in cyberspace where your site will reside. Examples of well-known internet hosts include EarthLink, NetPass, and Yahoo!, but there are many others to choose from. The main criteria to consider when choosing a host are how often the site goes down, how quickly it goes back online after experiencing downtime, and how long it's been in business. It's always best to choose a host that's well established so you can be fairly confident it will be there to serve you in both the near and distant future.

Web hosting prices have plummeted in the past few years. You can find reliable and reputable web hosting for as little as $3.95 per month for unlimited disk space. Some of the hosts also will allow you to register your domain name (discussed below) when you sign up, which saves you a step. But since web hosting is very competitive, it pays to shop around for the best deal. You can find a list of the top 10 hosting sites at webhostingchoice.com, plus you'll find a list of host names in the Appendix at the end of this book.

Naming Rights

Before you can sign up with a web host, you must select and register a unique name, known as a domain name (or URL). As with your business name, you'll want to use a name that best describes your business, such as davidjonesassociates.com. With a common name like David Jones, however, it's possible someone else is already using the name. The company that registers your name will check it against other registered names before giving you the go-ahead to use the one you've selected. For this reason, it's a good idea to have more than one name in mind when you're ready to register.

As with hosting, domain name registration is cheap-cheap-cheap—as little as $1.99 at GoDaddy.com, for instance.

Bright Idea

If you discover that the name you'd like to use as your domain name has already been taken, try it with a different extension at the end of your address. New extensions are always being created because of the huge number of websites activated every day. One to check out is the newly created ".us.com."

(Not so long ago, you could expect to pay around $70 for a two-year term.) There are several companies that can register your name, but one of the best known is domain.com, which offers domains as low as $9.75 per year. So what's with the difference in price? You'd have to read the fine print to figure it out. Your best bet is to ask your computer consultant for a recommendation, since he or she likely encounters plenty of different hosts and domain providers while working on customers' computer equipment.

For more information about online advertising and marketing, check out the "Net Sales" chapter in *Startup Basics*.

Stat Fact

Internet usage is just about evenly divided along gender lines, according to a recent Harris Interactive poll, although women have a slight edge at 51 percent. However, in terms of ethnicity, whites lead the pack by far, with 74 percent of the American adults who are online. Eleven percent of internet users are black, and 12 percent are Hispanic.

Internet Toolkit

While it's crucial to promote your business 24/7 with a professionally designed website, here are a number of other viral marketing tools available—all at no cost—that you can use to extend your marketing reach. Here's a rundown on these must-have cyber tools:

- *LinkedIn (linkedin.com):* This business-oriented social networking website was launched in 2003 to encourage professional networking. It now has 40 million members in 170 industries. LinkedIn is useful for establishing new contacts, reconnecting with old business acquaintances and friends, and finding new business.
- *Facebook (facebook.com):* Originally a social network for college students, Facebook has become a place for businesspeople to network. You can post a profile, photo, videos, and other information, plus people who visit can post comments. "Facebook allows you to get your brand out to a wide audience base in a short time," says Jason Brown, a Michigan PR consultant. "When I heard that in terms of size Facebook would be the seventh largest country in the world, that hit home for me. It helped me spread the word about my company, goals, and objectives a lot faster than if I hadn't used web channels."
- *Myspace (myspace.com):* This online community is a place where friends connect, but it's becoming another place for business professionals to hang, too. Its features are similar to those of Facebook.

- *Blogs:* Short for "weblogs," blogs are frequently updated personal online journals. They're either linked to an existing website or are floated in cyberspace using a blog template. Many entrepreneurs make money as bloggers by selling proprietary information (like books) or by selling advertising space.

- *Twitter (twitter.com):* This hot micro-blogging tool allows you to send brief (up to 140-character) messages, or "tweets," to anyone who subscribes. It's meant to update people on what you're doing, which of course is why entrepreneurs are using it. Brown scored a big PR coup after he "tweeted" the CEO of an online shoe store to tell him about his client's unique footwear. A short time later, the shoes were online. "Twitter is great because it gives you quick access to people who can sometimes lead to new business," Brown says.

So which of these tools should you use? How about all of them! "You need to have your name out there on as many service networks as possible," says Brown, who has the logos of three social networks on his website. "Once you see how they work out, you can focus on just three."

Website Design Questionnaire

The following questions, provided by Elbel Consulting Services, LLC, will help you determine how your website should look, what it should contain, and what features it should include. The answers also will help you convey this information to your website designer, who will need this information before he/she can produce a quality website according to your specifications.

1. Do you want a commercial, nonprofit, personal, or special issue website? _____

2. What line of business are you in?

3. What is the purpose of your website?

   _____ Disseminate information

   _____ Market your company and products

   _____ Sell products online

   _____ Build constituent and supporter base

   _____ Other _____

4. Is your business primarily internet-based?

5. How long have you been in business?

6. Where is your business in the marketplace?

   _____ Lagging _____ On par with competition _____ Leading edge

7. Who are your customers / clients / constituents?

8. What message are you trying to deliver to your customers / clients / constituents?

9. Who is your intended website audience?

10. How will people learn about your website?

11. What do you want people to do once they visit your website?

12. Do you have an overall marketing strategy?

13. How will you promote your website?

14. What marketing and website suggestions have you received?

15. Do you have existing marketing material that can be adapted for use on your website?

16. Which competitors' websites do you like and why?

17. Which competitors' websites do you not like and why?

18. Do you have an existing website? What are its good and bad features?

19. What kind of material will you include on your website?

_____ Information about us

_____ Contact us

_____ Marketing information

_____ FAQ

_____ Product information

_____ Store

_____ Journals

_____ Articles

_____ Current information

_____ Realty information and home listings

_____ Industry-specific information

_____ Personal material, writings, and accomplishments

_____ Political platform

_____ Other _____

20. Will your website content be oriented toward:

_____ Archival _____ Current _____ Mixed

21. How often to you plan to update the main pages on your website?

_____ Yearly _____ Quarterly _____ Monthly _____ Weekly _____ Daily

22. Who will update the visible (or "copy") on your website?

_____ Webmaster _____ Me _____ Both

23. Which features do you think will improve your website?

_____ Store

_____ Content management system

_____ Blog

_____ Bulletin board

_____ Photo gallery

_____ E-mail campaign manager

_____ Realty specific

_____ Audio

_____ Video

24. How complex will your website be?

25. How many pages will your website contain?

_____ 3–5 _____ 10 _____ 20 _____ 50 _____ 100 _____ 500+

26. How many visitors do you intend to draw to your website every week?

_____ Does not matter _____ 10 _____ 50 _____ 100 _____ 500

_____ As many as possible

27. Will your website reach out to returning or new visitors?

_____ Returning visitors

_____ New visitors

_____ Mixed

28. How important is it to keep people coming back to your website?

_____ Not important

_____ Somewhat important

_____ Very important

29. Do you want help creating website (or "copy")?

_____ No

_____ Some suggestions

_____ Some help

_____ Significant help

30. What image do you intend to convey?

_____ Solid, established

_____ Current

_____ Entrepreneurial, new

31. What website appearance are you looking for?

_____ Traditional

_____ Current

_____ Leading edge

32. What mood should your website convey?

_____ Mellow

_____ Friendly

_____ Energetic

_____ Emphatic

33. Do you want your website to look like others in your line of business?

_____ Same

_____ Somewhat different

_____ Unique

34. Do you prefer less expensive, plain design, or custom artwork and layout?

_____ Plain

_____ Somewhat customized

_____ Custom

35. What color scheme do you prefer?

_____ Solid, traditional, businesslike

_____ Hot

_____ Attention-getting

36. What role should graphics and photos play on your website?

_____ Minor

_____ Some

_____ Significant

37. Who will provide the materials and content? _____

_____

_____

38. Who will be responsible for reviewing and approving the website? _____

_____

_____

39. How will you measure your website's success? _____

_____

_____

40. What other guidelines do you have regarding your website? _____

_____

_____

_____

Money
Matters

N ow that we've explored the elements that go into establishing your consulting business, let's take a look at how you'll pay for them. In this chapter, you'll find out how to create a simple income and operating expense statement so you'll know how much money you need to make ends meet, then learn where you can get the cash you may need to finance your new venture. We'll also cover setting fees and how to get those checks rolling in.

Income and Operating Expenses

Keeping track of both income and operating expenses is crucial to the success of your business. Without a tool to track how much money you have coming in vs. the amount flowing out, you can quickly find yourself in financial trouble—trouble that can lead to the dissolution of your business.

Protect yourself by keeping track of all income and expenditures on a monthly basis. All you need is a simple income and operating expense (I&E) statement, which you can create easily using QuickBooks or a simple spreadsheet program like Excel.

We've given you two sample I&E statements on pages 126 and 127 that show the operating expenses for two hypothetical consulting businesses. The first business, Retail Management Consulting, is a sole proprietorship, and David Jones and Associates is an S corporation with one full-time employee (the owner) and one part-time administrative assistant. Both are homebased, so no office or utility costs are noted on the sample worksheets. We've estimated other projected monthly costs for each business to give you an idea of how much a new business might be expected to spend. Read on for details on what these costs entail, then plug in your own numbers on the worksheet on page 128.

Phone Charges

Despite the fact that cell phones are slowly killing off the traditional phone industry, there are some good reasons to install a landline ("wired line") as your business phone. To begin with, the cost has dropped dramatically. You can get a landline for about the same price (about $45 a month) as a cell phone plan. In addition, a landline business phone helps you to keep your business in the office where it belongs—and not in your pocket 24/7. Also, you get the highest-quality voice transmission and dropped calls are never an issue with a landline. Finally, you need a landline to run a home security system. And like a cellular phone, the cost of a line used exclusively for business is 100 percent deductible, so it makes sense to have one in your home office.

Extra features you'll need include voice mail, call waiting, and caller ID. Most phone companies include these as part of their monthly bundled service package, although you may have to pay a little extra for voice mail (usually around $2 to $5 a month).

> **Beware!**
> Don't try to make your residential landline or personal cell phone do double duty as a business line. It's unprofessional and a real business deserves to have real business tools. Besides, do you really want to take the chance that you'll answer "Wassup?" when your most important client calls?

If you add an extra line for your fax machine or modem, you may be able to get a multiline discount, so shop around for the best price. For the purpose of this exercise, we're using $90 to represent the cost of two phone lines with voice mail on both charts.

If your cell phone is used strictly for business, the cost can go on your I&E, too. As mentioned in a previous chapter, basic packages start at about $39.95 for hundreds of minutes of airtime and go up to as much as $99.99 for plans with unlimited minutes. We've inserted $40 on both charts.

Postage

As mentioned in Chapter 10, you'll probably want to send out direct mail a couple of times a year to entice new prospects to use your consulting services. First-class postage is currently 44 cents, which is the best way to mail materials you want someone to open and read, versus bulk mail, which often is perceived as junk mail. Because you'll probably be mailing out a lot of quotes, contracts, and reports, you should estimate extra postage costs to cover those, as well. You may find that the estimated $25 per month shown on the sample I&E is too low for your particular situation, so feel free to up the ante.

> **Beware!**
> While it's true that e-mail and text messaging have transformed business communication, you still should be prepared to mail contracts, proposals, and quotes if you're asked to. Some people are wary of opening e-mail attachments, so you'll need to include some funds in your monthly budget to pay for snail mail delivery.

Licenses

Unless you're doing work that requires you to have special licensing or certification (say, if you're a hazardous waste control consultant), it's likely the only licensing you'll need will be a standard business license. This type of license is issued by the municipality in which you're based, and the cost varies. For simplicity's sake, we've used $3 on our sample I&E, which would equate to license costs of $36 per year. And in case you're wondering: Yes, you should break out even the smallest costs like this one incrementally and include them on your operating I&E. After all, incremental charges do add up, and when totaled could amount to quite a bit of cash. Naturally, you won't be paying these costs in such increments. Rather, you'll set the money aside so next year, when expenses like your license fees come due, the cash will be sitting safely in an account somewhere.

Sample Operating Income and Expenses

Retail Management Consulting

Projected Gross Monthly Income		**$4,500**
Projected Monthly Expenses		
Mortgage/rent	$0	
Phone (landline)	90	
Cell phone	40	
Utilities	0	
Postage	25	
Licenses	3	
Owner salary	3,000	
Employee wages	0	
Benefits/taxes	335	
Advertising/promotion	100	
Legal services	20	
Accounting services	80	
Office supplies	50	
Insurance	125	
Transportation	100	
Magazine subscriptions	10	
Membership dues	20	
Loan repayment	0	
Online service	40	
Web hosting, domain name	5	
Miscellaneous	380	
Total Projected Monthly Expenses		**$4,423**
Projected Net Monthly Income		**$77**

Sample Operating Income and Expenses

David Jones and Associates

Projected Gross Monthly Income		**$6,000**
Projected Monthly Expenses		
Mortgage/rent	$0	
Phone (landline)	90	
Cell phone	40	
Utilities	0	
Postage	25	
Licenses	3	
Owner salary	3,000	
Employee wages	580	
Benefits/taxes	422	
Advertising/promotion	100	
Legal services	20	
Accounting services	80	
Office supplies	50	
Insurance	210	
Transportation	100	
Magazine subscriptions	10	
Membership dues	20	
Loan repayment	0	
Online service	40	
Web hosting, domain name	5	
Miscellaneous	480	
Total Projected Monthly Expenses		**$5,275**
Projected Net Monthly Income		**$725**

▲

Operating Income and Expenses Worksheet

Projected Gross Monthly Income $

Projected Monthly Expenses

Mortgage/rent $

Phone (landline) $

Cell phone $

Utilities $

Postage $

Licenses $

Owner salary $

Employee wages $

Benefits/taxes $

Advertising/promotion $

Legal services $

Accounting services $

Office supplies $

Insurance $

Transportation $

Magazine subscriptions $

Membership dues $

Loan repayment $

Online service $

Web hosting, domain name $

Miscellaneous $

Total Projected Monthly Expenses $

Projected Net Monthly Income $

Salaries

If you're a one-man band, it's easy to figure out what to put on your I&E—just estimate how much you'd like to earn in a year and divide that amount by 12 to get a monthly figure.

But what's a realistic amount? You could try using the figures mentioned in Chapter 2 from the Bureau of Labor Statistics. The BLS says that the median wage for management analysts who consult in the management, scientific, and technical fields was $35.37 per hour in 2008, or $73,570 per year, while the hourly mean wage was $46.35, which works out to $96,420 per year. No doubt you'd be thrilled to earn either wage, but the truth is, you're likely to have a lean first year until you become adept at marketing your services. A more reasonable estimate might be $36,000 a year, which would work out to 12 projects at $3,000 each—a doable number even for a neophyte consultant. So that's the amount that has been inserted into the Retail Management Consulting I&E for purposes of illustration. You will, of course, have to earn more than that to cover the cost of the two-person business, which is why we're assuming a higher projected monthly income amount of $4,000 on the other I&E.

Entry-level and clerical employees often start at the federal minimum wage, which currently is $7.25 per hour. Some states have their own minimum wage laws, so you should check with your state's department of labor for the current wage. On the David Jones and Associates I&E, we figured in a wage for a 20-hour-a-week administrative assistant at $7.25 an hour ($145 per week, $580 per month).

A more skilled employee, such as a consulting associate, would of course be paid at a higher rate, possibly as high as $20 per hour. Ask your business associates how much they pay their administrative staff to see what the market will bear.

> ## ▲ Beware!
> The IRS requires written records for any business expenses you deduct, including the cost of phone service or long-distance calls. Because it can be difficult to remember which phone numbers belong to which client on your itemized bill, keep a log of business calls that lists the date of the call, the company/individual name, and the phone number.

> ## Smart Tip
> _Tip..._
> It's usually a wise idea to live below your means during the startup phase of your consulting business. While you'll have to cover your everyday living expenses, you may find that making a few financial sacrifices now could benefit the business tremendously later.

Fringe Benefits and Taxes

As you'll recall from Chapter 7, offering benefits can be a good way to retain good help. But the fact is, many small-business owners can't afford to offer much more than perhaps a one-week paid vacation or the occasional sick day. So although benefits do make people happy, it's not always necessary to offer them. But if you decide to offer benefits like medical insurance, you can assume that your cost will be 8 to 10 percent of the employee's hourly income.

One thing that's not negotiable is payroll taxes. As you know from Chapter 7, there are a whole slew of taxes you'll have to pay on employee wages, including the FICA tax, federal unemployment tax, state unemployment tax, and workers' compensation insurance. Since you don't have previous records to compare to, you should estimate high so you're not caught short. Your accountant can help you make a reasonable guess.

Incidentally, if you're using subcontractors (aka independent contractors), they're fully responsible for their own taxes. Just make sure you comply with the IRS's definition of independent contractors. (As we mentioned in Chapter 7, IRS Publication 15-A, Employer's Supplemental Tax Guide, can give you more information about the employee/independent contractor distinction.) To make things simpler, we've calculated employee taxes, etc., at 15 percent ($87) for the David Jones I&E and haven't included any money for benefits. Then there are the taxes you'll pay as a sole proprietor on your own earnings, beginning with estimated taxes. The IRS requires you to make quarterly estimated tax payments on your income, and in fact will charge you a hefty penalty if you don't pay enough in the quarter in which the taxes are due. But as you can imagine, estimating taxes when you're starting a new business can be tricky. Consult with your accountant for help, or if you want to simplify matters, take your projected income, multiply it by 40 percent, and send that amount in, divided appropriately between Uncle Sam and your state's treasury department. (You can find out what your state's current tax rate is by contacting the treasury department.) If that sounds really high, you're right—it is. And one reason why it's so high is because the federal government assesses a self-employment tax on entrepreneurs, which is the other half of the Social Security and Medicare taxes. (Remember, you're the employer of record, so you have to foot the entire bill.)

If you form an S corporation, you're also required to pay estimated taxes on any money you earn, even if all the money stays in the corporation. While the top federal corporate tax rate for an S corporation is 35 percent, you could pay less, depending on the amount you earn and the number of deductions you're eligible for.

It should be pretty apparent that tax issues can be very complex. We strongly recommend that you consult your accountant to make sure you're paying enough taxes and paying them on time. What will an accountant cost? It's safe to estimate that you'll use an accountant no more than about two to three hours a month. The BLS says that in 2008 the national median hourly wage for accountants was just under $27.50, so for the sake of simplicity, we've used $80 per month on the sample I&E to cover a few hours of accounting services.

Office Supplies

You'll need a variety of supplies every month, including pens, legal pads, report covers, computer paper, and other supplies. For other expenses like business printing that aren't incurred every month, add up the figures you arrived at for your startup expenses worksheet in Chapter 6 and divide them by 12 to get a estimated figure for your I&E. We've used $50 on both sample I&Es.

Advertising

These expenses can add up, so you'll want to estimate them as closely as possible. Don't forget to include the cost of producing direct-mail pieces, newspaper advertising, and any other business awareness efforts you may decide to do, as well as your Yellow Pages advertising costs. You should also include your publicity costs (like for news releases) here just to make things simple. You'll find a figure of $100 on both of the sample I&Es.

Insurance

If you did the insurance exercise in Chapter 5, you already have a pretty good idea of how much business and personal insurance you'll need. Tally the cost of the annual premiums, divide that by 12, and plug that number into your I&E. Our figures of $125 and $210 are culled from the estimated annual costs—$1,500 and $2,500, respectively—from the sample startup expenses chart in Chapter 6.

Transportation

As a consultant, you're likely to be on the road a lot. So this is the place to figure in the cost to run and maintain your vehicle, including gasoline, tune-ups, windshield wiper fluid, oil changes, and other motoring costs like tolls. If you're consulting in an urban area that has a reliable transportation network, like New York City, Washington, D.C., or Seattle, you'll want to include your subway, bus, or other transportation costs on this line instead. For the purposes of our sample I&E statement (and the amount might be totally off target for you), we've estimated $100 per month to represent the cost of driving for business.

Magazine Subscriptions

As discussed in Chapter 8, magazines and trade publications are a good way to stay current on issues of importance to you and your clients, so you'll probably want to subscribe to a number of general and specialty consulting publications. Include 1/12 of their cost on your operating statement. We've chosen to use $10 per month, or $120 a year.

Membership Dues

Among the types of membership dues you'll want to include here are the costs to join industry-specific organizations and local business organizations like the chamber of commerce. Refer back to Chapter 8 for a list of the major organizations that service consultants. For the sake of illustration, we've included membership dues of $20 per month on the David Jones and Associates chart only.

Loan Repayment

If you purchased a vehicle for use in your business, the loan payment figure goes on your monthly expense report. This is also where you'd include repayment of any loans from family, friends, and investors, if applicable.

Internet Service Fees

Internet connection fees vary widely. Here's a recap of the approximate amounts you can expect to pay:

- *Standard ISP:* $10 to $20 per month
- *DSL:* $30 to $40 a month
- *Cable modem:* $40 a month, plus basic cable TV service, at the minimum
- *Broadband high-speed satellite internet:* $30 a month

We're assuming a cost of $40 per month on each I&E, as well as $5 per month to cover the annual cost of web hosting and a domain name.

> **Beware!**
> The IRS won't object if your family vehicle doubles as business transportation as long as you keep careful written records on the number of miles you drive for each purpose. You're allowed to deduct only the percentage of the insurance costs, the loan payment, maintenance, gasoline, etc., that pertains to the business.

Other Miscellaneous Expenses

It's always a good idea to add 10 percent of the bottom line total to cover miscellaneous expenses, some of which won't crop up until you've actually started consulting.

Financing Your Startup

One of the great things about being a consultant is that you really don't need much cash to launch your business. For instance, Costa Mesa, California consultant David McMullen started his computer business for just a few hundred dollars, which was all he needed to buy a few office supplies, business cards, a computer repair kit, and a new briefcase. For this reason, many consultants use personal savings or plastic to buy a new computer and the other supplies needed to open for business. But let's say you're thinking big and you need more cash to buy a building or purchase a specialty piece of equipment. Then you'll undoubtedly need to obtain financing to make your dreams a reality.

Other sources of financing include:

- *SBA:* This government agency offers a number of different loan programs, as well as free counseling and training. See the "Fed Funds" chapter in *Startup Basics* for more information.

- *Unsecured personal loan:* This type of loan is usually much easier to obtain than a business loan. Important note: Good credit is a must to qualify.

- *Personal capital:* Sometimes it pays to tap into your own resources rather than to ask someone else for a buck, since it saves on finance charges and preserves your peace of mind. In fact, funding a startup out of personal savings, as both Schiavone and Susan Bock did, is often the preferred choice for many aspiring consultants because the amount required to launch the business is so low.

"One good thing about paying out of personal savings is that you can stay solvent when business is off because you don't have loans to pay back," Schiavone says. "The business climate has been treacherous for me since 9/11 because most of my customers cut back on marketing. I also had a couple of big contracts end when the person I was dealing with left the company.

Tip...

Smart Tip
Because it can be difficult for an aspiring entrepreneur to obtain a large startup loan, it may be wise to start your consulting business as a side job while you're still employed full time. This allows you to both set aside money for the startup and establish a record of success that will impress your banker.

Having no overhead and no loans to repay meant I could make it through the bad times."

"Just be sure to have sufficient funds to sustain the business for several months," Bock adds. "The ability to sustain yourself is a crucial element in your success because business can be cyclical, and since often no two years are the same it can be hard to predict your income stream."

> **Tip...**
>
> **Smart Tip**
>
> As a new business owner you won't have a track record of success, so your best bet is to approach small financial institutions like community banks if you need financing. You also may find that credit unions generally are more willing to consider a request for startup capital.

- *Home equity line of credit (HELOC) loan:* Your bank may not be willing to give you a HELOC for a business startup, but it's worth asking.

- *Credit cards:* This is a popular choice for many entrepreneurs. Just spend wisely. You don't want to start your new career with a huge amount of debt hanging over your head.

- *Family and friends:* To avoid losing a friend or breaking up a family over money squabbles, handle the transaction in a professional, businesslike way. That includes putting the terms in writing, offering a fair interest rate, establishing a repayment schedule, and making payments on time. Your bank would expect no less, so you should extend the same courtesy to your family and friends. See the "All in the Family" chapter in *Startup Basics* for information about how to ask for and structure this kind of loan.

How Much Should You Charge?

Have you heard the one about the newspaper printing plant that's in serious trouble because its presses stopped running due to a mechanical malfunction? Unless the presses start again within the next few hours, the newspaper won't be on the newsstands when the sun comes up. The repair people on the job are stumped and can't figure out why the presses have stopped working. So they call in a consultant, not worrying about the high fee they know they'll be charged because of the late hour. It doesn't matter, because the first priority is to get those presses running again.

The consultant comes in, takes a few minutes to examine the printing press, then goes over to one of the gears and taps it with a wrench. Within seconds, the presses resume rolling, and the papers make it to the newsstands in the nick of time. When the consultant submits his bill for $1,005, he's asked why he is charging such an odd amount. "Simple," he replies. "The $5 is for tapping the gear and $1,000 is for knowing which gear to tap!"

Bill Me

Consultants often find themselves puzzled about how to set fees. They feel guilty if they set them too high, but they also know they may not be able to stay in business if they set them too low.

To survive as a consultant in any industry, you need to charge fees that will enable you to stay in business; at the same time, both you and your clients need to feel that your fees are fair and equitable. Always remember that as long as you have clients who are willing to pay for your services and your fees are reasonable (and comparable to others in the industry), you have reached the so-called "middle ground" when it comes to fee structures. For help setting your fees, contact the membership organization that services the industry in which you work and ask what their research shows. Then sit back, relax, and enjoy cashing those checks.

So when you set your fees, remember that people are willing to pay you for knowing which gear to tap! If you charge too little, you won't succeed in business. If you charge too much, you won't get any clients. So how do you find that middle ground that seems fair to everyone involved? One way to help you decide how much to charge is to find out what the competition's rates are. A simple telephone call to ask for their brochure and rates or a visit to their website should do the trick. Then set your rates so you're competitive with everyone else in the community.

Smart Tip

It's a good idea to establish a relationship with a local banker even if you don't need startup capital. You never know when you might need a short-term loan to complete a project, such as interior design work or the purchase of expensive new equipment.

Before setting your fees, make sure you've considered all your potential expenses. There's nothing worse than setting your rates, having your client pay you on time, then finding out you failed to include several expenses. This brings up an important point to remember in every job you take from a client: Include a "miscellaneous" line item in your fee proposal. But don't pad the miscellaneous figure to earn additional income. That's unprofessional, as well as unethical.

Keep one important rule in mind when establishing your fees: The more money people pay for a product or service, the more they expect to get for their money. In other words, if a client agrees to your hourly rate of $400, then you had better give $400 worth of service every hour you work for that client.

When setting your rates, you have several options, including hourly rates, per-project fees, and working on a retainer basis. Let's examine each one.

Hourly Fees

You need to tread carefully when setting hourly fees because two things could happen:

1. Your hourly rate is so high that no one could ever afford you (therefore no client will ever knock on your door).

2. Your hourly rate is so low that no one will take you seriously. Some clients prefer to be billed on an hourly basis, while others hate the idea of paying someone what they perceive to be too much per hour. Such clients usually prefer to pay per project, which we'll discuss shortly.

> ### Dollar Stretcher
> When you print your brochure or other information about your consulting business, don't include your rates. Instead, print your prices on a special insert. That way, you can change rates without having to reprint the entire brochure.

> ### Beware!
> Don't set your fees too high; you may pick up a few clients in the beginning, but unless your rates are competitive—and fair—you'll fail miserably as a consultant.

Bear, Delaware fundraising consultant John Riddle has had many clients who asked to be billed on an hourly basis. Since all those clients were nonprofit organizations, it became clear that because a board of directors was ultimately responsible for the financial health of those agencies, they were more comfortable working with a fundraising consultant who charged by the hour. It makes it easier for some nonprofits to determine their actual fundraising costs when an hourly billing system is used.

Project Rates

When working on a project rate basis, a consultant normally gets a fixed amount of money for a predetermined period of time (a situation known as "work for hire"). But trouble can arise when the final tally—especially if it's a large one—is presented to the client. Riddle decided to head off that problem by billing monthly, until he realized that some of his fundraising clients were paying late. He solved that problem by asking clients who wished to be billed on a monthly basis to pay the first and the last month's fees at the contract signing, then wouldn't start work until he had the check in hand. That helped tremendously to keep the cash flowing.

Retainer Basis

Working on a retainer basis gives you a set monthly fee in which you agree to be available for work for an agreed-on number of hours for your client. While in the ideal world you would have a dozen or so clients who hire you and pay you a hefty sum each month (then never actually call you except for a few hours here and there), don't get your hopes up. Most companies that hire a consultant on a retainer basis have a clause in their contract that prohibits him or her from working for their competitors.

Working and getting paid by this method certainly has its advantages. You're guaranteed income each month, which helps with cash flow when you're starting out in your consulting business. Some consultants actually offer a percentage reduction in their fees if a client will agree to pay a monthly retainer fee. Riddle, the Delaware consultant, says the average retainer is $3,500 per month.

Bonus Options

It's common for consultants to have some type of bonus option in their clients' contract or letter of agreement. A bonus may be a percentage of an amount that the consultant saves a client (if the consultant has been hired to reorganize a department or division, for example) or the amount of money acquired for a client (as in the case of fundraising, collections, or grant writing). Here's how the latter can work to your advantage, according to Riddle: "When a client offered to pay a percentage of any money I raised for the organization, I counteroffered and asked for a small monthly retainer fee instead," he said. "I also took a cut in the percentage rate they originally offered. This way, I would receive something each month for any work I did, but I was still guaranteed a bonus."

In the end, Riddle charged the client $2,000 per month for 12 months, or $24,000 in retainer fees for the year-long contract. He also earned a bonus of $17,000, which was 10 percent of the $170,000 he raised. If he had accepted the client's initial offer of 20 percent of the funds raised, he would have earned only $34,000 rather than the $41,000 he earned by restructuring the deal.

Although it's not always possible to work out this kind of deal, it never hurts to negotiate. If you do, keep in mind that the average bonus is 15 to 20 percent of the funds obtained for the organization. For more information on quoting prices, see the "On the Money" chapter in *Startup Basics*, where you'll also find a sample worksheet you can use to make the quoting process easier.

Billing and Collections

It's easy to get into a cash flow crunch very quickly if you don't bill on a regular basis. One way to make sure money is always coming in from your clients is to build a payment schedule into your contract. Typically, consultants request a partial payment on the first of the month for the duration of the contract if they're on retainer; or half upfront and half at the end of the contract if they work on a per-project or hourly rate. Others, like Schiavone, prefer to wait until the work is completely finished before asking for payment.

"I prefer to be sure that my customer is completely satisfied before I send a bill," she says.

When it comes to getting those bills out, Bock recommends sending invoices electronically rather than on paper, since it gets them into the hands of the client faster. QuickBooks has an invoicing function to make creating those invoices easier.

What happens when the check's not in the mail? Collections are an unavoidable part of doing business. It's not uncommon for companies and individuals to ignore your stated terms or to stretch them out as long as possible before paying. Still others won't pay until *after* you've started collection proceedings like sending reminder bills and placing collection calls.

To avoid collection problems, it is a good idea to ask for one-half of your fee up front, particularly when you're dealing with a new client. You should also include clearly stated payment terms in your contract, like specifying that full payment is due on delivery of the agreed-on work.

Today's accounting software packages, including QuickBooks, include collection management tools to streamline the collection process. In fact, QuickBooks by Intuit is a good choice for all your accounting needs. The Pro version retails for $199, and you can use it to generate invoices and estimates, track receivables, write checks, pay bills, and more. It's particularly useful because it interfaces seamlessly with Microsoft Office Accounting, Excel, and TurboTax. You can find QuickBooks at office supply and computer stores.

> **⚠ Beware!**
> Pay quarterly taxes on your earnings, including bonuses. Otherwise you could be in for a real shock (as in an underpayment penalty) if you wait until April 15 to pay tax on any substantial earnings you receive from your clients.

Should You Accept Credit Cards?

Depending on your line of work, you may be able to command a large fee for your expertise. For this reason, you may wish to consider accepting credit cards for the services you provide. It can be an especially good idea to offer this payment method if you offer workshops or seminars, or if you sell subscriptions to a newsletter. Research has shown that people won't hesitate to plunk down their charge card to buy something at a seminar or trade show. But those same people more often than not will hesitate to write a check for that product or service.

The Check's in the Mail

Here are five ways to keep the checks coming in while you're between jobs:

1. *Write articles for your local newspaper.* Virtually every newspaper in the United States buys material from local freelance writers. And since you're a professional in your chosen field, you should have no difficulty writing articles for those newspapers. Such articles enhance your portfolio and impress potential clients.

2. *Write articles for trade journals relative to your niche.* For instance, if you're a marketing consultant, send articles to marketing journals and magazines. Consider the publications to which you have subscriptions as good candidates for your material. But don't stop there; check out *Writer's Market* (Writer's Digest Books) in your local library for more leads.

3. *Work for a temporary employment agency.* Depending how much time you have available, you may choose to work for a few days or a few weeks just to keep money coming in. But if you choose this route, don't forget to keep marketing your services.

4. *Teach a course at your local college.* Check with your local college's employment office to see if there are any openings for an instructor for the noncredit courses offered. If there are no openings for instructors, consider offering a new course. Another option for teaching a workshop is to offer one free of charge. You may not get paid, but you'll get free publicity for your business.

5. *Write a book.* Did you know that it's possible to sell a book idea on the basis of an outline and a sample chapter? Writer's Digest Books (writersdigest.com/books) has several excellent tomes that explain how to get published. By writing and having a book published about the industry in which you consult, you'll add credibility to your work as a consultant.

To accept credit cards, you'll need a merchant account, which is a clearinghouse for electronic payments, a point of sale (POS) terminal, and a receipt printer or receipt software for your computer. There's a whole raft of service charges associated with a merchant account, which can be hard to take and annoying to manage when you start your business. But if you really want to offer a credit option and you don't want the hassle of setting everything up yourself, consider using PayPal. This service costs a little more than a standard merchant account, but you don't need any hardware or software to run it. For information about PayPal, go to paypal.com.

For in-depth information about accepting credit cards, check out the "Charging Ahead" chapter in *Startup Basics*.

Avoiding Cash Flow Problems

So far we've discussed your *potential* for making money. But it bears mentioning that many consulting businesses fail because they experience too many cash flow problems. Cash flow problems affect both large and small businesses every day in this country, so don't feel bad if you run into some temporary cash crunches.

Here are a couple ways to avoid the cash flow blues:

- *Before you sign a contract or letter of agreement, make sure you've double- and triple-checked the budget you've proposed.* Go over each line item and expense carefully, because the time to spot trouble is before it begins.

- *Consider asking for the first and last month's fees up front (at the signing of the contract), or at least ask for one-third of the amount you expect to collect.*

> **Tip...**
>
> **Smart Tip**
> When accepting credit cards, think beyond MasterCard and VISA. Your clients may prefer to use American Express or the Discover card. Check with your bank, PayPal, or other merchant account provider to see what credit card options are available.

This, of course, will depend on who your client is, how healthy his or her organization's cash flow situation is, and so on. If your clients have failed to keep up their end of the payment schedule, refuse to continue working until payments have been brought up to date. Make sure you have a clause in your contract or letter of agreement addressing this problem; otherwise, a client may have you over a legal barrel.

Writing Winning
Contracts and
Reports

Now that you've laid the foundation

for your new consulting business—or you're started working

on the tasks discussed in this book, at the very least—it's

time to think about two important tools you'll need to be an

effective consultant: the consulting contract and the client

report. In this chapter, we'll deal with the mechanics of con-

tract writing and report generation and give you tips on how

▲

to put together materials that will win you jobs, turn clients into repeat customers, and induce those clients to refer you to everyone they know.

Simply put, a contract is a legal document between two or more parties that involves what attorneys call "an exchange of value." That is, if something of value (money, goods, services) is provided in return for something else (in your case, consulting services), then the agreement is considered to be a contract. And it doesn't matter if the task or service you're performing is quick and easy, or complex and time-consuming. You must always, always protect yourself by creating a contract that the client will sign. After all, this is your livelihood at stake, and if something goes wrong you'll need solid legal documentation to make sure you get paid.

By the way, contracts should always be written. Why? Because it is difficult, if not impossible, to enforce a verbal agreement. You've probably heard tales about contracts hastily written on the back of matchbooks or on cocktail napkins. Even those types of notes are preferable to a verbal agreement sealed with a handshake because they're more likely to be taken seriously in a court of law if a legal dispute arises.

Contracts protect both the contractor (notice that there's a "contract" in the word "contractor") and the client. To make sure there are no misunderstandings, you must be sure that every contract you write is clear, specific, and detailed enough to cover all the important points or clauses. Your contracts should be written in plain language, which is clear and easily understood prose. This doesn't mean, however, that you don't need an attorney to look over your contracts or help you create a template you can reuse. It does mean that you don't have to impress anyone with whereases, heretofores, and other legal gobbly-gook.

In addition to spelling out all the terms of your agreement, a contract can help you avoid what Susan Bock, the Huntington Beach, California consultant, calls "project creep," in which you begin with a specific task that morphs into more work than you agreed to as the project proceeds. Having a signed contract that details exactly what you've agreed to do will help you rein in projects before they take on a life of their own.

Contracts can be very simple one-page documents, or they can be 100 pages long or more, depending on the subject matter and how many complicated issues they cover in depth. They also can take the form of a letter of agreement, which is shorter and less formal but is just as binding as a formal contract. You'll find a sample contract and a sample letter of agreement that you can use as idea-starters on pages 150 to 153.

Contract Contents

Here's a short list of what should be included in every consulting contract:

- *Full names and titles of the people with whom you are doing business*—and be sure they're all spelled correctly.

- *Project objectives:* Making a list so you can check it twice—or thrice—or even more often will help you achieve the project goals and help you figure out when the job is done and you can stop. ("Project creep" can go both ways.)

- *Detailed description of the project:* Write a global description that specifies every aspect of the task you've been asked to do.

- *List of responsibilities:* Record exactly what you will be expected to do or the major steps you'll take to complete the project. It can be helpful to create a list of checkpoints you can refer to as you work. You might also want to have the client sign off on each phase of the project to ensure his/her satisfaction with the work as it progresses. If so, the sign-off process should be included as an item on your list of the responsibilities.

- *Fees:* In addition to mentioning the agreed-on fee, you can include a payment structure (i.e., the percentage of the fee that's due at certain points of the work process). You'll find some advice on how to figure out your fee a little later.

- *Timeline:* Specify the start and end date of the project, and indicate any pertinent dates in between (including those dates on which you wish to have the client sign off on your work in progress and/or payment dates).

- *Definition of important terms:* This might include industry-specific terms, or other terms that you'll use in the commission of the job.

Smart Tip

Let your contract or letter of agreement rest for 24 hours before you sign on the dotted line, especially if your client has asked you to revise or add to the contract you've drafted. Sometimes a good night's sleep will help you see the details in a whole new light.

- *Page numbers:* This might sound pretty basic, but the idea is to keep the client—or you, for that matter—from adding pages to the contract that not everyone has agreed on.

This is not an all-inclusive list. Your attorney may recommend including other information, such as legal definitions, legal recourse in the event of nonpayment, nonperformance clause (as in what will happen if either party reneges on their obligations), and so on. This is just one more reason why it's a good idea to have your legal eagle draw up your contracts or give the ones you write the once-over before they're presented to clients.

Fun Fact

One of the earliest types of contracts was created by the ancient Romans. Known as stipulatio, this type of oral contract was created in question and answer form. As a result, a man who couldn't speak couldn't enter into a stipulation—resulting in one more good reason why written contracts are better than oral.

Setting Fees

Of course, before you can turn over those contracts, you'll have to figure out your minimum monetary requirement for each project. The first rule in the consulting business is to be flexible. Sometimes, you'll find a client really, really wants to hire you, but can't pay your entire fee. Depending on the situation, you may want to reduce your fee, either so you can get some much-needed experience or because you believe you can set yourself up for more work in the future by working cheaper now. But don't sell yourself short; make sure you're paid what you're worth, since that fee sets the tone for future fee negotiations. The figure you arrive at should include compensation for your time, and compensation for your business overhead, such as travel, office expenses, and so on. But when quoting a figure, leave room for some negotiation, because sometimes clients will ask you to reduce your rates by a set amount or a few percentage points to meet their budget. Just be sure you have a bottom line figure in mind when you sit down to negotiate so you know how much wiggle room you have.

At the same time, don't try to wring out the highest possible fee from your clients. You want to be fairly compensated, but if your fee is too high you run the risk of losing the business completely. "To stay in business, you can't let your fee structure rule," stresses John Riddle, the Bear, Delaware fundraising consultant.

> **Beware!**
> Listen to your intuition. If something doesn't feel right about what a client wants or expects, make sure every point is clarified in your contract or letter of agreement. Leave nothing to chance.

Types of Fee Structures

Consultants can set fees in many ways. Among the most common are:

- *By the hour:* Consultants often calculate a project cost based on the number of hours they expect to spend on it. To figure out an appropriate hourly rate, you can either use a source like the Careers in Consulting website (careers-in-business.com) to see what consultants earn in your area, or decide how much you'd like to earn in a year and do the math to turn that figure into an hourly rate. For example, if you'd like to earn $60,000 per year, divide that by 52 weeks to get approximately $1,154 per week, then divide that by 40 hours a week to arrive at an hourly rate of $28.85. Experienced consultants often double or triple the resulting figure to cover overhead, benefits, and other expenses. And if you think about it, a consulting rate of $40 to $60 isn't out of line when you consider the expertise you're offering.

By the project: It can be a little tricky to determine a project rate when you first start consulting because you don't have historical information on which to base your hourly estimate. But once you figure out how many hours you think the job will take, simply multiply that figure by your hourly rate, then add 10 percent or so to cover unexpected contingencies.

- *By the day:* If you know approximately how many days the project will take, a day rate makes sense. No tricky math here—just multiply your hourly rate by the number of hours you expect to work over the specified number of days.

- *On a retainer basis:* A retainer is a set amount of money paid on a regular basis (usually monthly) to use the services of a business professional as needed. For instance, you might work for the client eight hours one month, but only three the next, but you still earn the same amount of money each month. This kind of fee arrangement is common for computer consultants and other providers of ongoing services.

Going the Extra Mile

No matter which fee structure you select, you must strive to meet your clients' needs fully and complete projects on time. It's also your responsibility to make sure clients feel that they're getting the full value for their money. One way to do this is to bring the project in a little under budget. You don't actually have to take a loss on the project; rather, quote just a little higher at the outset, then present a bill that comes in under that amount, yet fairly represents the amount of time you've spent on the project. Clients will appreciate the gesture and likely will think favorably enough of you to call you for another project or refer you to their colleagues.

Bright Idea

To give your important correspondence the weight it deserves, send documents to your clients via courier or overnight delivery service. Using the USPS's Priority Mail service also makes your documentation look important.

In addition, it's not uncommon for clients to ask to have additional services performed—without cost to them, of course (the dreaded "project creep"). So when negotiating, keep in mind that clients may secretly hope that you'll be able to provide them with some type of extra service, and add a little extra time to your initial estimate to accommodate such requests. Riddle does this routinely when working with fundrais-

Smart Tip

Tip...

In your report, specify who's going to be responsible for each task; unless you specify in writing who's doing what, both you and your client may assume that the other person will be doing the work that's required.

▲

ing clients, since they often hint that they would love to have additional information on potential funding sources. Because they're usually reluctant to pay for extra research time, he quotes a higher fee for the services they contract for and is able to provide the additional data at what appears to be no charge. That kind of goodwill gesture ends up costing you nothing but is invaluable for creating future business prospects.

The Fine Art of Negotiating

Of course, before you get to the point where you need to write a contract, you have to sit down with the client and negotiate project details, from timelines to fees. Always prepare in advance by reading up on the company before you arrive

> **Beware!**
> Before you present a contract to your client for a signature, be sure to proofread it carefully—a couple of times, if possible. Nothing says "amateur" more than a document full of typos, misplaced punctuation, or grammatical errors, plus it certainly won't inspire confidence in your abilities in the mind of your client.

(historical financial info is a must), and always have a general fee range in mind when you sit down with your potential client. You can feel free to adjust the amount upward or downward after you've heard the details of the project.

The overall negotiating process can be difficult and even intimidating for a new

Contract Pointers

In addition to the details discussed earlier, every contract has three key elements that must be present for the contract to be valid:

- *The contract must contain an offer.* An offer is simply something proposed by a person or business. For example, an offer for one of John Riddle's fundraising clients may include language like this: "... JR will act on behalf of the XYZ nonprofit organization as a fundraising consultant to raise the necessary funds required for ..."
- *Each contract must contain acceptance.* Acceptance is when one party accepts the terms offered in the contract. It's usually a good idea to put a time limit on any contract or letter of agreement you offer a client. For example, you might state that the offer will expire in a set number of days unless it is signed and accepted.
- *Each contract must contain consideration.* This is the amount you'll be paid. For example, the contract language could say something like "... in exchange for a monthly payment of $5,000."

consultant. So here are a few tips that will boost your confidence when negotiating contracts, as well as help you make a favorable impression on your client:

- *Smile and relax.* Take a deep breath, and don't sweat the small stuff. Remember, if you look relaxed and happy, your client will be, too.

- *Make your first impression count.* How many times have you met people and, for whatever reason, decided you would rather have nothing to do with them? Well, the same holds true in client–consultant relationships. First impressions count. So make yours an excellent one.

- *Go to the meeting prepared.* Your client will probably ask you some questions to test your knowledge of the subject in which you claim to be an expert. So make sure you're up to date on the latest information in your field.

- *Be ready to listen.* The true test of your listening skills will take place at the initial client meeting. This is where your clients will talk about what they really want and when they expect it to be accomplished.

- *Take plenty of notes.* Information will be flying right and left across the room. Take accurate notes because your contract or letter of agreement probably will be based on the notes you take during the initial meeting.

- *Ask plenty of questions.* Only then can you accurately determine what the client wants and expects. To determine what to ask, see the worksheet on page 154.

It's the Law

Once you have a signed contract and you've received that first partial payment, then you're home free, right? Not necessarily. The law says that either party can terminate a contract if any of the following has taken place:

- *Duress:* Neither party may use force or pressure—and that includes both the mental and physical kind—to get the contract signed.

- *Fraud:* If either party intentionally misrepresents her- or himself or something they promise to deliver (or pay for), then fraud is present. And when fraud is present, the contract can be null and void.

- *Legality:* The contract you're about to sign must be for a transaction that's legal. For example, if a fundraising consultant stated in a

> **Beware!**
> You should have a contract for every consulting assignment you undertake, even if you're working for a previously satisfied client or someone else you know. When money is involved, friendships and relationships can sour very quickly where there's a disagreement, so make sure everything that's expected of you is put into writing.

▲

Setting the Tone

T he first client-consultant meeting sets the tone for the entire relationship. Here are some important things to keep in mind when you go to that first meeting:

- *What is your client's personality?* Does your client have an aggressive, take-charge management style? Or is the client more of a "let's get to know each other before we do business" type of person? The sooner you discover your client's personality, the easier it will be for you to get the job done.
- *What's your client's problem?* Does your client even know what the orga-nization's problem is? Or are you being asked to investigate the problem and come up with the solution? More often than not, a client will have a good idea about the problem and how to solve it. Make sure you agree with your client on what the real problem is before you agree to accept a contract.
- *Is your client ready to accept your recommendations?* Make sure your client has an open mind and is willing to listen to your recommendations.
- *Can you agree on a timetable?* Although most clients would like you to solve their problems in a few days, most are reasonable when it comes to giving you the time you need to solve those problems. However, you'll sometimes run into clients who have a hard time understanding why you can't solve their problems overnight. Unless you can convince clients at the initial meeting that a reasonable timetable needs to be agreed on, you might want to reconsider signing a contract with them.
- *Can you outline who will take responsibility for each task?* Make certain that everything is spelled out in writing and that the contract clearly states who is responsible for each task.

contract that he or she would use any means necessary to raise the funds they need—including stealing, if the need presented itself—then the contract would be null and void.

- *Capacity:* Each party who enters into the contract must be of legal age and sound mind, and not under the influence of alcohol or drugs. (Surely no consultant would sign a contract under those conditions, but who knows?)
- *Full disclosure:* If either party fails—on purpose—to disclose a key piece of infor-mation, the contract will be unenforceable.

Reporting Your Findings

Once you've completed a job to the client's satisfaction, it's time to report your findings. This serves two purposes. First, it demonstrates to your client exactly what you've done and how you've fulfilled the requirements of the contract. Second, it serves as a written record of your activities that can be used as an idea starter for future work. However, as we mentioned in a previous chapter, it's never a good idea to try to use a report written for one client as a boilerplate document for all the others that follow. After all, clients and their needs differ, and since they're paying the big bucks for your expertise and imagination, they deserve to have a report tailored to their specific situation.

Having said that, there's no reason why you can't look at other consultants' reports for inspiration, since having a firsthand look at how consultants present their solutions and how they format the documents can be helpful when you write your own reports. For this reason, we've included a sample consulting report beginning on page 156, which was prepared by John Riddle for an actual client.

Read through it to get an idea of one way to attack the report-writing process. As a consultant, you'll also need to provide periodic written updates to your client. These help keep the lines of communication open and avoid potential problems. Your update can be as simple and direct as the sample beginning on page 159.

And there you have it—everything you need to know to establish your business, create comprehensive contracts, and write winning reports. The rest is up to you. Happy consulting!

Tip...

Smart Tip

Write several drafts of your final report for your client, polishing your ideas and expanding on them as you go. Keep the writing simple—choose simple words over complex words, and use plenty of bulleted lists to emphasize your main points.

▲

Letter of Agreement

[on company letterhead]

5/31/09

Client Name
Company Name
Street Address
City, State, ZIP

Dear Client name,

Thank you very much for hiring MarketWise Insights, Inc.. to conduct research for the
_____ **project**. As we discussed, the project will include the following:

Item	Includes
Develop research tool	Could include development of data model, market share model, discussion guide, or survey
Conduct research	Research detail
Data analysis	Data analysis detail
Final research output	Deliverable detail, such as write research report or provide data model, market share analysis, market forecasts, research summary, presentation

The first phase of this project will begin on *Date* and the estimated completion date is *X* months from that date. While every effort will certainly be made to complete the project in this timeframe, the client understands that delays may occasionally occur and agrees that MarketWise Insights, Inc. cannot be held responsible should those delays occur. In the event of such delays, MarketWise Insights, Inc. will work with the client to develop a new acceptable schedule.

To facilitate the project, the client, *client name*, will
- Provide the discussion guide
- Recruit participants (i.e., identify correct participant, and speak/e-mail with them beforehand to secure participation in the research; provide more names as needed)
- Be available for consultation for the duration of the project
- Distribute incentives to participants

The compensation for the project will be:

[on company letterhead]

Schedule and conduct up to 10 interviews	= $ *xxxx*
Write research report	= $ *xxxx*
Total	= $ *xxxx*

Note: Additional interviews beyond 10 will be billed at $*xx* per interview.

Payable as follows:

- Payment 1 (50% of total) at contract acceptance $*xxx*
- Payment 2 (50% of total) at project completion $*xxx*

Payments should be made payable to MarketWise Insights, Inc. Carol Monaco will submit invoices to the client, and payment terms are Net 30 days. Please note that late payments may be charged interest at the prevailing rate. Of course, the client or MarketWise Insights, Inc. may terminate at any time with 30 days' notice, and the amount charged will be prorated based on the estimated completion date.

The Client, *client name,* agrees that marketing and market research are inexact sciences, and as such, agrees that Carol Monaco and MarketWise Insights, Inc. shall not be held liable for the recommendations that may or may not prove to be exact over time. It is understood that any recommendations arising from this project are based on Carol Monaco's expertise and best available knowledge at that time, and as such, are recommendations and forecasts, and may or may not prove to be true depending on market conditions and other circumstances.

I'm delighted to be working with you again and look forward to beginning this project. If you agree with the details outlined in this letter, please sign it and fax a copy to me at (303) 123-4567. I will sign it and fax it back to you for your records. If you have any questions, please give me a call at (303) 123-4567.

I agree to the above terms and conditions,

_____   _____

Client Name   Carol M. Monaco
Client Title   President
Company   Marketwise Insights, Inc.
Street Address
City, State, ZIP

_____   _____

Date   Date

▲

Sample Contract

This is an agreement between [name of consultant] ("CONSULTANT") with offices at [address, city, state, ZIP] and [name of client] ("CLIENT"), with offices at [address, city, state, ZIP].

CONSULTANT agrees to provide public relations consultation and program implementation to CLIENT as mutually agreed on in Attachment I.

In consideration of the services described above, CLIENT agrees to pay CONSULTANT $_____ for the professional public relations services in Attachment I. Expenses incurred to satisfy this agreement are incremental to the professional fees as outlined in Attachment I and will be billed as incurred or billed directly to CLIENT. Invoices will be issued the first of each month and are payable on receipt.

CLIENT shall be responsible for expenses associated with CONSULTANT's provision of the services, such as travel, copies of clips and/or videotapes, and distribution services, as well as out-of-pocket costs such as general office expenses, including duplicating, phone, fax, postage, FedEx, etc. CONSULTANT will not commit to any expenditure of $_____ or more without prior approval of CLIENT.

CONSULTANT agrees to obtain the approval of CLIENT before releasing information to the public. All materials created, assembled, and prepared by CONSULTANT pursuant to this agreement shall be subject to CLIENT's approval. The CLIENT agrees that such approval or disapproval will be promptly given to CONSULTANT on request for same.

In connection with performance of the services, CLIENT may disclose to CONSULTANT or CONSULTANT may otherwise discover information that may include, but is not limited to, technical, financial, or business information. Such information shall be deemed to be proprietary (Confidential Information); however, Confidential Information shall not include information: (1) previously known to CONSULTANT free of any obligations to keep it confidential or (2) publicly known through no act of CONSULTANT. CONSULTANT agrees that he shall hold all Confidential Information in confidence and shall not make any disclosure of any such Confidential Information to anyone except those of CLIENT's employees to whom such disclosure is necessary for the purposes authorized by this Agreement.

All materials created, assembled, and prepared for CLIENT are the property of CLIENT, including finished and unfinished materials.

CLIENT warrants that the information, photographs, artwork, and all other materials it provides to CONSULTANT in connection with this project will not in any way constitute an infringement or other violation of any copyright, patent, trademark, trade secret, or other proprietary rights of any third party. Accordingly, CLIENT shall defend, indemnify, and hold CONSULTANT harmless from and against all liability, damages, loss, cost, or expense (including but not limited to reasonable attorney's fees and expenses) arising out of the breach or alleged breach of its warranties or representations hereunder.

CLIENT shall defend, indemnify, and hold harmless CONSULTANT from and against any and all claims, liabilities, damages, losses, and expenses, including the reasonable fees of experts and attorneys and all costs of suit, suffered or incurred by CONSULTANT (the "Claims") arising out of (i) the Agreement, (ii) the performance by CONSULTANT of his responsibilities under the Agreement, or (iii) the sale or use of any product made, distributed, or sold by CLIENT, including, but not limited to, Claims for personal injury or death relevant to this project.

CONSULTANT has the right to publicize the relationship between CONSULTANT and CLIENT in the media. CLIENT will have the right to approve the announcement before it is distributed.

The laws of the State of *State* shall govern this agreement. In case of a dispute related to or arising out of this agreement, both parties agree to refer the dispute to a recognized dispute resolution group. If mediation does not resolve the issues outstanding, the dispute will be referred to the American Arbitration Association. CONSULTANT and CLIENT agree to abide by the decision of the Association.

If any provision of this agreement is declared void or otherwise unenforceable, such provision shall be deemed to have been severed from this agreement, which shall otherwise remain in full force and effect. This agreement contains the entire agreement of the parties with respect to the obligations, representations, conditions, or inducements, oral or otherwise, of any kind whatsoever. No change or addition shall be made to this agreement except in writing executed by the appropriate representatives of the parties. Failure of either party to enforce its rights under any provision of this agreement shall not be construed as a waiver of that party's right to enforce such provision(s) in the future. Nor shall any waiver of any breach of this agreement be held to be a waiver of any other or subsequent breach.

All notices required or permitted to be given under this agreement shall be in writing. IN WITNESS WHEREOF the parties, by their appropriate officers, duly authorized to bind their respective companies, have executed this agreement as of the date and year first written above.

By:

_____   _____

                                                Date

_____   _____

                                                Date

Courtesy of Donna K. Ramer/StrategCations Inc.

20 Questions

What better way to learn what your clients want and expect (and how much they are willing to pay for your expertise) than to ask questions? Here are 20 questions you should ask a potential client before signing any contract or letter of agreement:

1. Can you define the problem you're experiencing?

_____

_____

2. How long has the problem affected your business?

_____

_____

3. Have you taken any steps on your own to solve the problem?

_____

_____

4. Why do you think the problem is occurring?

_____

_____

5. What are your overall objectives on this project?

_____

_____

6. How do you think your problem can be solved?

_____

_____

7. Is your organization committed to solving the problem?

_____

_____

8. Is your organization ready to implement suggested changes?

_____

_____

9. Who will be my designated liaison on this project?

_____

_____

10. When is the latest date you would like to have this project completed?

_____

_____

11. When is the earliest date you would like to have this project completed?

_____

_____

12. What will be your role during the project?

_____

_____

13. Who will supply me with all the data I request?

_____

_____

14. Have you developed a budget to pay for the changes I recommend?

_____

_____

15. How much have you budgeted to pay for a consultant?

_____

_____

16. Will I be working with any confidential or restricted documents?

_____

_____

17. How often can we meet?

_____

_____

18. Can meetings be called as necessary?

_____

_____

19. How often would you like progress reports?

_____

_____

▲

20. When would you like me to begin?

_____

_____

By the time you've asked your clients these 20 questions (and recorded their answers), you'll have all the information you need to draft your contract or a simple letter of agreement.

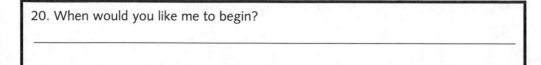

Sample Consulting Report

Fort Delaware Society
Fundraising Report

After carefully studying the Fort Delaware Society's position as a nonprofit agency in the State of Delaware, the following fundraising plan has been drafted for your review. It's recommended that the board of directors carefully review each item, and decide if, and when, it would like to proceed. Although no fundraising plan is ever guaranteed or foolproof, this one has been designed to raise $26 million for the Fort Delaware Society over the next three years.

1. Private Foundation Support: $24 million

Delaware's largest foundations include Longwood, Welfare, Laffey-McHugh, Marmot, Crystal Trust, Delaware Community Foundation, Sharp Foundation, Beneficial Foundation, and Life Enrichment Foundation. The top foundations—Longwood, Welfare, Marmot, Laffey-McHugh, and Crystal Trust—should be solicited for a total of $3 million a year over three years. The remaining Delaware foundations should be solicited for a total of $1 million per year over three years (total: $12 million).

Other foundations that have a history of funding projects like the renovation and restoration of Fort Delaware include Pew Charitable Trusts, AT&T Foundation, Fidelity Foundation, Chrysler Foundation, Merrill Lynch Foundation, Abell Foundation, Newman's Own Foundation, F.M. Kirby Foundation, Allegheny Foundation, Cafritz Foundation, Andrew Mellon Foundation, Stern Foundation, Wray Trust, Heinz Endowments, J. Paul Getty Trust, and the Turner Foundation. There are dozens of others, but these should be contacted first. Collectively, you should request $4 million per year over three years (total: $12 million).

Note: Fort Delaware Society also qualifies to request money from additional foundations that participate in the National Standard Grant Application. These foundations have joined together to make the application process simple. Once a master application has been received, an agency can make copies and send them to the appropriate foundations on the list. After carefully reviewing the list, it looks as if Fort Delaware Society has an additional opportunity to solicit 70 foundations. Amounts range from $25,000 to $2 million.

Recommendation: Beginning in November, start soliciting funds from the Delaware foundations, the national foundations, and the foundations on the National Standard Grant Application list.

2. Corporate and Business Support: $1.75 million

Partnerships between nonprofit agencies and businesses are slowly beginning to mature and take important directions. While it's the normal procedure to solicit a corporation or small business for a contribution, it's suggested that Fort Delaware Society set itself apart from the other nonprofits that are constantly sending letters asking for "just a handout." Instead, Fort Delaware Society should devise a program known as the "Adopt the Fort" plan. This plan consists of asking corporations and small businesses to "adopt" a section of the Fort. The "adoption" process involves not only monetary contributions but also providing volunteers and in-kind donations. (For example, suppose First USA Bank adopts the Fort for one year. It may donate $20,000 and supply volunteers from its employee committees. Companies may also contribute other items on your wish list, as needed. They would also be in a position to host a picnic for their employees at the Fort, thereby increasing the number of visitors and increasing Fort Delaware Society's mailing list.)

These types of "adoption" plans have been successful with schools and businesses throughout the country. Few other nonprofit agencies have yet to try this approach; Fort Delaware Society has an opportunity to be on the cutting edge and lead the way in Delaware with a new approach to corporate and business giving.

Recommendation: Beginning in January, start soliciting the top 500 corporations and small businesses in New Castle County to participate in the "Adopt the Fort" plan. (I have the list of the 500 top corporations and businesses.)

Important Note: Random surveys were taken during the past 90 days, and, unfortunately, out of 1,000 people surveyed, only 167 had ever heard about Fort Delaware or Pea Patch Island. By implementing the "Adopt the Fort" plan, hundreds of thousands of Delawareans would be exposed to the Fort.

3. Special Events: $150,000

A "Walk for the Fort" event should be held in the fall (mid to late September). Because of the uniqueness of Pea Patch Island and the Fort, this type of walkathon should attract approximately 1,000 walkers. Each walker would be required to raise a minimum of $100 to qualify for an incentive prize (T-shirt, sport bottle, etc., with the Fort Delaware logo and logo of the corporate sponsor that provides the prize). Additional money can be raised through other sponsorship opportunities (signage, refreshments, entertainment, etc.). This daylong event will again raise greater awareness of the Fort among the general public.

Recommendation: For this event to be a success, a walk committee should be formed no later than January 15. I can provide an entire how-to kit, which lists the steps necessary to hold a successful walkathon.

4. Miscellaneous: $100,000

Other ways to generate fundraising dollars include:

- *Direct mail:* Using both the current Fort Delaware Society mailing list and a new prospect list, solicit funds with a two-page letter and an information sheet about the Fort. (Start this campaign in March; I will supply a new prospect list.)
- *Sponsorships and advertising:* Offer corporations an opportunity to advertise at the Fort when it is open. Many businesses would be willing to pay top dollar to have their signs, banners, etc., at such a unique location. This is fairly easy to implement: Simply contact advertising agencies in the tri-state area, and they will take care of selling the idea to their clients.
- *Sale of pieces of property:* (On paper only, of course!) Just in time for the holidays, people will be able to give a unique gift to their loved ones. No more fruitcakes, ties, slippers, etc. Instead, for only $25, they can buy a certificate (printed on old-time parchment paper, to look like it has been around awhile) that says they own a "piece of property." This has worked well with people who "buy" stars out of the sky and receive only a certificate with their name on it. The pieces of property could be sold in a variety of ways: at the mall, from your website, on QVC (home shopping network, always looking for something "different"), or at selected gift and novelty shops in the area. You could even market them through schools and nonprofit agencies and offer them the opportunity to make $5 on each certificate they sell. You would receive less money, but you would make up the difference in volume.

Sample Consulting Update Report

By mid-September, the research for your Capital Improvement Campaign should be completed. The research will be divided into several categories: Foundations (Delaware, regional, and national), Corporations, and Small Businesses. In addition, we will explore the possibility of holding a major special event next year.

Delaware Foundations: The following foundations in Delaware accept requests for contributions from qualified 501(c)3 organizations.

	Average Grant Amount
Beneficial Foundation Inc.	$25,000
Bernard A. & Rebecca S. Bernard Foundation	$20,000
Chichester duPont Foundation Inc.	$35,000
Crestlea Foundation	$25,000
Crystal Trust	$40,000
Delaware Community Foundation	$10,000
Ederic Foundation	$50,000
Fair Play Foundation	$30,000
Good Samaritan Inc.	$15,000
Kent-Lucas Foundation	$15,000
Milton & Hattie Kutz Foundation	$10,000
Laffey-McHugh Foundation	$50,000
Longwood Foundation	$250,000
Life Enrichment Foundation	$15,000
The Lovett Foundation	$15,000
Marmot Foundation	$50,000
Sharp Foundation	$35,000
Welfare Foundation	$75,000

It is strongly suggested that the Possum Point Players submit a request to each of the above foundations for a capital grant. Over the course of the next several weeks, I will prepare additional detailed information concerning the address, deadlines, and what information is required for each application.

Recommendations for the next 30 to 45 days:

- Continue researching other sources of foundation funds. (John Doe)
- Start compiling your mailing list, and make sure it includes vendors, present and past contributors, and patrons. Also, have all board members start making lists of people they know (business contacts, relatives, friends, church acquaintances, etc.). These lists will be added to a database of people who can be solicited for a donation. (Board)
- Develop several special event ideas. (John Doe)
- Develop a list of noncapital funding resources. (John Doe)

Glossary

Advertising specialties: Promotional products that may be personalized with a business name and are intended to bring visibility to the company when the item is used; also known as "trinkets and trash"

Blog: A frequently updated online journal used as personal diary or—for a business owner—to spread the news about your company; short for "weblog"

Blogosphere: A term coined to describe the entire blog "universe"

Corporation: A form of business ownership that protects the owner's personal assets against potential business losses

dba: Acronym for "doing business as," which refers to any name chosen as a business name, including those that include the owner's name (as in David Jones and Associates)

Domain name: The address of an internet network (for example, entrepreneur.com)

Facebook: Social networking site that consists of a directory of people's names and includes photographs and personal information (facebook.com)

Flash: An electronic file format used on a web page that consists of graphics and/or animation; also known as Shockwave Flash

Footprint: The amount of space something (typically electronic equipment) occupies

Insurance broker: An insurance agent who sells the products of many different insurance companies

Letter of agreement: A simple contract in letter form

LinkedIn: A business-oriented social networking site (linkedin.com)

List broker: An individual who acts as an agent between a list provider and potential list buyers

LLC: Limited liability company, a type of legal business entity

Lumpy envelope: A direct mail piece that includes a small gift; the idea is to pique the curiosity of the recipient enough to open the envelope

Merchant account: An account established through a bank or other financial institution in order to receive payments by credit cards, e-checks, and other forms of payment

Netbook: Mobile device used for internet access to e-mail, social networking sites, weather, videos and photos, and other leisure activities; although it looks similar to a laptop computer, it has fewer capabilities

News release: A one- to two-page article, often on company letterhead, used to generate favorable publicity; also known as a press release

Partnership: A business owned by two or more persons, or partners, in equal or unequal proportions

PayPal: Internet-enabled system for the secure transfer of payments between businesses and customers (Paypal.com)

Plain language: Proposed in 1998 by the Clinton administration, plain language refers to language in government documents that's clear, concise, easy to read, and logically organized; applicable to any other type of writing as well; also known as plain English

ProfNet: An online network of business professionals who offer their expertise to journalists looking for sound bites or interviews (profnet.com)

Project creep: Uncontrolled changes in or additions to a project that result in extra work and aren't part of the original agreement; also known as "scope creep"

Retainer: Fee paid on a regular basis (often monthly) to use the services of a professional when needed

SCORE: Nonprofit organization dedicated to offering no-cost business services to entrepreneurs and small-business owners (score.org)

Social network: Online community of people who share the same interests; Facebook is an example of a social network

Sole proprietorship: A business owned by one person

Twitter: Social networking site that functions as a "micro-blog," or online journal for updating your friends or associates (known as "followers") about activities and thoughts; messages are 140 characters long or less and are called "tweets"

Unsecured personal loan: A loan that doesn't require collateral

Viral marketing: Using social networks like Facebook or Twitter to advertise and increase brand awareness

Web hosting: Type of service that allows individuals and organizations to place a website on the internet so it can be viewed by multiple users

Appendix: Consulting Resources

They say you can never be too rich or too thin. While those points could be argued, we believe you can never have too many resources. Therefore, we present for your consideration a wealth of sources for you to check into, check out, and harness for your own personal information blitz.

These sources are tidbits, ideas to get you started on your research. They are by no means the only sources out there, and they should not be taken as the Ultimate Answer. We have done our research, but businesses tend to move, change, fold, and expand. As we have repeatedly stressed, do your homework. Get out and start investigating.

Attorney Referrals and Information

American Bar Association
abanet.org

Find an Attorney
findanattorney.com

Lawyers.com
lawyers.com

Martindale-Hubbell Law Directory
(800) 526-4902
martindale.com

Business Software

Adobe Dreamweaver CS4
Adobe
(800) 833-6687
adobe.com

Microsoft Office
available from most computer and office supply stores, including Staples, Office Depot, OfficeMax, and many other retail and online stores

QuickBooks Pro
Intuit Inc.
(877) 683-3280
quickbooks.intuit.com

Peachtree Pro Accounting
Sage North America
(877) 495-9904
peachtree.com

Consultants

Jeff Bartlett
The Bartlett Group Inc.
(717) 540-9900
bartlettresearch.com

Susan Bock
Susan Bock Solutions
(714) 847-1566
sbocksolutions.com
Susan@SusanBockSolutions.com

Jason Brown
PublicCity PR
(248) 252-1687
publiccitypr.net
jbrown@PublicCityPR.net

Fred Elbel
Elbel Consulting Services
elbelconsultingservices.com

David P. McMullen
McMullen Consulting
mcmullenconsulting.com
info@mcmullenconsulting.com

Bill Metten
Bill Metten and Associates
(302) 234-9936

Carol Monaco
MarketWise Insights, Inc.
(303) 659-8061
marketwiseinsights.com

Melinda Patrician
Melinda Patrician Consulting
4229 S. 36th St.
Arlington, VA 22206
(703) 824-1765

John Riddle
(302) 834-4910
johnriddle@sprintmail.com

Merrily Schiavone
AdHelp Graphic Design Services
(302) 366-0681
adhelp.biz
merrily@adhelp.biz

Consulting Organizations

American Association of Healthcare Consultants
(888) 350-2242
aahc.net
info@aahcmail.org

Association for Consulting Expertise
(800) 464-5043
consultexpertise.com

Association of Management Consulting Firms
(212) 551-7887
amcf.org
info@amcf.org

Association of Professional Communication Consultants
consultingsuccess.org

Association of Professional Consultants
(800) 745-5050
consultapc.org
apc@consultapc.org

CMC-Canada
(416) 860-1515, (800) 268-1148
cmc-canada.ca
consulting@cmc-canada.ca

Independent Educational Consultants Association
IECA National Office
(703) 591-4850
educationalconsulting.org
info@IECAonline.com

Institute of Management Consultants USA
(800) 221-2557
imcusa.org

Professional and Technical Consultants Association
(408) 971-5902, (800) 74-PATCA
patca.org
info@patca.org

Public Relations Society of America
(212) 460-1400
prsa.org
membership@prsa.org

Society of Professional Consultants
(978) 692-6950
spconsultants.org
contact@spconsultants.org

TechServe Alliance
(703) 838-2050
techservealliance.org

Consulting Publications

Consultants News
BNA Subsidiaries LLC
(603) 924-6390, (888) 259-1500
consultingcentral.com

Consulting Magazine
BNA Subsidiaries LLC
(215) 788-8505
consultingmagazine.com
consultingmagazine@icnfull.com

Inside Consulting
insideconsulting.com

Kennedy Consulting Research & Advisory Wire
BNA Subsidiaries LLC
register.consultingcentral.com

Management Consulting News
managementconsultingnews.com

Education/Training/Certification Resources

American Century University
Management Consulting graduate program
(505) 889-2711
centuryuniversity.edu
century@centuryuniversity.edu

CMC-Canada
(416) 860-1515, (800) 268-1148
cmc-canada.ca
consulting@cmc-canada.ca

Hawai'i Pacific University
hpu.edu

Institute of Management Consultants USA
(800) 221-2557
imcusa.org

Government Agencies

Minority Business Development Agency
(888) 324-1551
mbda.gov

U.S. Department of Labor
(866) 4-USA-DOL
dol.gov

Incorporation Kits

Inc. Plan USA
(302) 428-1274, (800) 462-4633
incplan.net

Quality Books
(305) 724-7463
qualitybooks.com
admin@contact-qualitybooks.com

Limited Liability Information
Limited Liability Company Center
limitedliabilitycompanycenter.com/states

Merchant Accounts

Capital Merchant Solutions Inc.
(877) 495-2419
takecardstoday.com

Credit Card Processing Services
(888) 717-1245
ccps.biz
Kevin@ccps.biz

InfoMerchant
(971) 223-5632
infomerchant.net

Merchant Accounts Express
(888) 845-9457
merchantexpress.com

Total Merchant Services
(888) 871-4558
merchant-account-4U.com
info@21cr.com

Merchant Account Alternatives

PayPal
PayPal.com

Office Supplies, Forms, and Stationery

Amsterdam
(800) 203-9917
amsterdamprinting.com

Office Depot
officedepot.com

OfficeMax
officemax.com

Paper Direct
(800) A-PAPERS
paperdirect.com

Rapidforms
(800) 257-8354
rapidforms.com
service@rapidforms.com

Staples
staples.com

Online Postage

Pitney Bowes
pitneyworks.com

Stamps.com
stamps.com

U.S. Post Office
usps.com

▲

Zazzle
zazzle.com

Printing Resources

ColorPrintingCentral
(800) 309-3291
colorprintingcentral.com

NextDayFlyers.com
(800) 251-9948
nextdayflyers.com

PrintIndustry.com
(703) 631-4533
printindustry.com
info@printindustry.com

Printing for Less
(800) 930-6040
printingforless.com
info@printingforless.com

Print Quote USA
(561) 451-2654
printquoteusa.com

Promotion Xpress
(888) 310-7769
proxprint.com

PSPrint
(800) 511-2009
psprint.com

Small Business Development/ Entrepreneurship Organizations

Ladies Who Launch
(440) 247-2239
ladieswholaunch.com

National Federation of Independent Business
(800) 634-2669
nfib.com

Small Business Administration
(800) U-ASK-SBA
sba.gov

Small Business Development Centers
sba.gov/sbdc

SCORE
score.org

Suggested Reading

Complete Idiot's Guide to Consulting
Robert Bacal
Alpha Books

The Business of Consulting: The Basics and Beyond
Elaine Biech
Pfeiffer

The Consultant's Calling: Bringing Who You Are to What You Do
Geoffrey M. Bellman
Jossey-Bass

Duct-Tape Marketing: The World's Most Practical Small Business Marketing Guide
John Jantsch
Thomas Nelson

The Entrepreneur's Guide to Writing Business Plans and Proposals
K. Dennis Chambers
Praeger

How to Succeed as an Independent Consultant
Herman Holtz and David Zahn
John Wiley & Sons

Million Dollar Consulting: The Professional's Guide to Growing a Practice
Alan Weiss
McGraw-Hill

Persuasive Business Proposals: Writing to Win More Customers, Clients and Contracts
Tom Sant
AMACOM

Smarter Consulting: How to Start Up and Succeed as an Independent Consultant
Mike Johnson
FT Press

Value-Based Fees: How to Charge—and Get—What You're Worth
Alan Weiss
Pfeiffer

Tax Advice, Help, and Software

H&R Block
handrblock.com

IRS
irs.ustreas.gov

Intuit TurboTax for Business
intuit.com

Telecom Companies

AT&T Business
(866) 816-3815
att.com/business

Carolinanet (Residential VoIP)
(336) 346-6000
https://carolinanet.nuvio.com/html/

Sage Telecom
(866) 385-7281
sagetelecom.net

Toll-Free Numbers
AT&T
(877) 490-1971
businessesales.att.com/products/product_tollfree.jhtml

Qwest Communications
qwest.com

Web Hosting/Domain Names

DOMAIN.com
domain.com

EarthLink
earthlink.net

GoDaddy.com
godaddy.com

HostMonster

hostmonster.com

SBC Webhosting.com

webhosting.com

Yahoo!

yahoo.com

Index

Index